IMAGINATION AND ETHICAL IDEALS

SUNY Series in Ethical Theory
Robert B. Louden, Editor

IMAGINATION
AND
ETHICAL IDEALS

Prospects for a
Unified Philosophical and
Psychological Understanding

NATHAN L. TIERNEY

State University
of New York
Press

Cover art work: *Study of a Head,* Florentine, School of Leonardo, XV'th Century. Chalk Drawing. Disegno n.425e, Collection Uffizi, Florence. Reprinted by Permission of la Direzione, Gabinetto Disegni e Stampe Daglio Uffizi.

Published by
State University of New York Press, Albany

© 1994   State University of New York

Production by Susan Geraghty
Marketing by Theresa Abad Swierzowski

Printed in the United States of America

For information, address State University of New York Press,
State University Plaza, Albany, N.Y., 12246

Library of Congress Cataloging-in-Publication Data

Tierney, Nathan L., 1953–
    Imagination and ethical ideals : prospects for a unified
philosophical and psychological understanding / Nathan L. Tierney.
        p.   cm. — (SUNY series in ethical theory)
    Includes bibliographical references and index.
    ISBN 0–7914–2047–7 (alk. paper). — ISBN 0–7914–2048–5 (pbk. :
alk. paper)
    1. Ethics. 2. Imagination (Philosophy)   I. Title. II. Series.
BJ1031.T54   1994
170—dc20   93–37146
                                                                CIP

10 9 8 7 6 5 4 3 2 1

CONTENTS

PREFACE

Our present inquiry does not aim, as our others do, at study; for
the purpose of our examination is not to know what virtue is, but
to become good, since otherwise the inquiry would be of no benefit
to us.

Aristotle, *Nichomachean Ethics*[1]

This book had its origin in a growing sense of disquietude about
ethical theory that I have felt over the last two decades. Moral
philosophers have achieved some substantial theoretical results,
and a number of intellectual confusions about ethics have been
impressively resolved. And yet, these studies seemed to have very
little connection with the lives that people are actually striving to
lead. I could not help but believe we have strayed far from the
intention Aristotle proposes above.

How had theory become so far removed from practice? The
effects are evident but the causes are obscure. Not that there is a
lack of suspects—every ideology in our ideological age has its
favorite villain—but eventually I have settled on two. Firstly, ethical theorists have placed too much reliance on the concept of universal principles, a consequence of the excessive attachment of
modern philosophy to the scientific notion of rationality articulated from the seventeenth century onward. Secondly, ethical theory has increasingly separated itself from other studies of the
human subject—most notably moral psychology and psychoanalytic studies of the self.

This book is a constructive attempt to fill those gaps. *Imagination and Ethical Ideals* is an interdisciplinary work which
investigates some of the links between moral philosophy and
moral psychology, with implications for both personal ethics and
social philosophy. It is grounded in a theory of ethical ideals, considered as products of the imagination. The argument of the book
is that the place accorded to the notion of principle in ethics has
been excessive. Over-reliance on it has given an air of unreality to

philosophical attempts to lay bare the rational and conative grounds for ethical behavior.

What seems to be missing is an adequate account of the passage, within the structure of the person, between theoretical understanding and concrete psychological motivation to ethical action. This is the constructive purpose of this book. It undertakes to reconfigure the space of ethical inquiry, so that the distinguishing characteristic of the ethical is to be found neither in purely theoretical formulation, nor in serviceability toward practical aims, but in the peculiar space between them. This space inherently implicates the structure of the self with the process of reasoning, including the self's motivational dynamics. So conceived, it becomes apparent that advances in ethical understanding require advances in self-knowledge which go beyond the abstract intelligibility of theory. Moral meanings are unique: in addition to intellectual clarity, they require insight of a more therapeutic (from the Greek *therapeuein*: to nurse, serve, or cure) kind, which alters life and action. Such a perspective puts the concept of moral authority in a new light, treating it as residing primarily within the developed individual, and only secondarily in the force of principle. If this is correct, it behooves us to try and understand those processes by which individuals become morally mature—*not* as an illustrative adjunct to our moral theorizing, but as the touchstone of moral meaning. Only thus can we know which theories are best to live by.

NOTES ON TERMINOLOGY

The terms "morality" and "ethics" have been given a variety of meanings by philosophers. Sometimes they have been used interchangeably; sometimes they have been distinguished in terms of logical level or domain of application. Sometimes "morals" has been restricted to universal principles while "ethics" referred to the concrete norms of the community (e.g. Hegel's *Sittlichkeit*). Sometimes both "morals" and "ethics" have been used very broadly to refer to anything that has to do with actions, passions or settled character (Cicero is often credited with coining the Latin *moralis* as a translation of the Greek *ethos*, meaning "custom" or "habit"). Sometimes "ethics" has been used to refer to that for which the individual's private conscience is responsible, while "morals" has been given a more public tenor. Sometimes the reverse has been meant. Sometimes "ethics" has been reserved for one's actions as part of a profession or sub-group of a community: we speak, for instance of medical ethics and legal ethics, but rarely of American ethics.

I shall use the terms "ethics" and "morality" more or less interchangeably. At most, I will vary them for emphasis—"morality" tending to refer more to the norms and customs of one's community, while "ethics" will tend to refer to the individual's response to social morality in terms of reflective engagement, valuation, and choice. But I stress that these two words are meant to denote two sides of a coin, or two dimensions of a single domain. Ethics and morality define a domain of thought and action stemming from (and reflecting on) our respect, responsibility and concern for persons.

One of the main problems that faces anyone seeking moral understanding today is that most of the central terms of our moral vocabulary—such as will, freedom, soul, desire, reason, and choice—seem to be the displaced survivors of a world view which has been largely been abandoned because of advances in other areas of knowledge. They appear as the lost children of a folk psychology containing not a few anachronistic presuppositions, ranging from a dualistic metaphysics of mind and matter to antiquated faculty psychology. Few people acquainted with philosophy would be willing to continue to endorse these presuppositions without radical modification. Relevant work in cognitive psychology, artificial intelligence, neurobiology etc. offers exciting glimpses of a future integration, but this is probably decades or (more likely) centuries away from providing the new richly integrated theoretical and practical vocabulary which the development of moral thought requires.

Since we don't yet have replacement terms with the same wealth of semantic connection, philosophical underpinning, or practical convenience, it seems pointless to abandon this vocabulary. Folk psychology may be ragged, but it is the best we've got for purposes of moral understanding; and it can be improved. This book is written, then, in a *pro tem* spirit: it does not seek to replace folk psychology, but to make it more intelligible.

I take this opportunity to thank New York University's School of Continuing Education for providing a grant which contributed toward the completion of this work. I would also like to thank my father Dr. Len Tierney, a teacher of the practice of social work, who taught me in a thousand ways that practice is the best and richest source of theory.

PART 1

Imagination in Ethics: Philosophical Aspects

CHAPTER 1

Contemporary Dilemmas in the Project of Ethical Understanding

> Imagination, a licentious and vagrant faculty, unsusceptible of limitations, and impatient of restraint, has always endeavoured to baffle the logician, to perplex the confines of distinction, and burst the inclosures of regularity.
>
> Samuel Johnson, *The Rambler*[1]

THE FAILURE OF THE ETHICS OF PRINCIPLE

Introduction

Moral philosophers since Socrates have put their trust in reason—rather than the authority of tradition or supposed revelations from divine sources—as the best guide to right conduct and living well, for traditions may become corrupt or be rendered anachronistic, and divine sources have a notorious history of equivocation, ambiguity, and duplicity. Even those whose faith in the divine had somehow survived the shocks of experience still needed to decide which gods to trust: the necessity to understand could never be abrogated for very long. For as Socrates attempted to explain to a baffled Euthyphro, it is not enough to agree that some actions are dear to *all* the gods; we must still understand what it is about those actions which makes them dear to the gods.[2]

Yet reason's work in understanding human action contained its own uncertainties and has required regular reinterpretation throughout history. To most of the ancients moral wisdom was a matter of either discovering a timeless Platonic essence of justice or conforming to an Aristotelian *telos* (natural end) of human life. To the medievals, usually working within one or other of these two ancient conceptions, it was a matter of making as intelligible as possible theological presuppositions which ultimately were accepted on faith. Today, these notions of timeless essence and natural *telos* have not well withstood the force of centuries of criticism. And while the enmity between faith and reason has perhaps abated somewhat since the early modern period, they maintain, at best, an uneasy truce.

The moderns, from the seventeenth century on, chose instead to tie their notion of rational authority to that of science, especially to that of scientific law or principle. The formal features of valid moral principles began to be specified and elaborated theoretically: generality of form, universal applicability, disinterestedness, publicness, and overridingness. The purest expression of this approach is Kant's deontological ethics: an action is moral if it is done for the right motive, namely out of duty—i.e., out of respect for the moral law. And Kant could go so far as to call this purely formal principle of universal law "the supreme principle of morality": "Act only on that maxim that you can at the same time will that it should become a universal law."

Utilitarianism, while relying on a material definition of the good (whether pleasure, the general welfare, the maximal satisfaction of preferences, or various forms of ideal end), is still a principle-based theory in its conception of the right: that action (or rule of action) is right which is justified by the principle of producing the greatest good (happiness, pleasure, welfare, etc.) for the greatest number of people.

Of course it was recognized that these formal absolutes, although they worked quite well in the schoolroom, worked less well in the full human world complicated by subjective viewpoints and the historical uniqueness of events. Still, general principles seemed to apply for the most part, and this was enough for most people most of the time. Those practice professionals, such as priests and school teachers, who needed an account of when and why apparently universal moral principles did not apply in certain cases could consult the detailed, if unacademic, manuals of casuistry.[3]

Academics for the most part disdained casuistry and continued to explore the domain of the ethical in a theoretical way, clarifying and deepening key moral concepts such as authority, autonomy, and impartiality. At the same time, however, an increasing air of unreality began to surround philosophical attempts to lay bare the rational grounds for ethical behavior. Too often, moral theorists seemed engaged in a kind of duplicity whereby they claimed to be fully convinced by their own principles (*pour encourager les autres?*) but were unable, in concrete terms, to communicate the rational ground of that conviction to others.[4]

Part of this neglect of the concrete context of moral problems has no doubt been due to the professionalization of philosophy. Distinctions which began as useful fictions for purposes of analysis have been elevated into a professional creed. Today, undergraduate students are quickly taught the distinction between descriptive ethics (the study of the moral values that people actually hold), normative ethics (the hortatory enunciation of moral norms and precepts with the aim of persuading people to be more ethical), and meta-ethics (the study of the logic of moral principles and the meaning of ethical terms). After a few brief gestures, descriptive ethics is quickly passed over to the province of anthropologists, psychologists, and sociologists. Normative ethics is rarely regarded as a legitimate academic activity at all and is usually left to popular moralists and religious preachers. Meta-ethics alone has been embraced by many as the only legitimate province of philosophy.

Along with this professionalization, there has been a growing separation of ethical theory from ethical practice. A non-initiate who naively picked up a professional journal of ethics in the hope that it might provide some moral guidance would quickly become perplexed and frustrated. Many ethical theorists have expressed some concern over this, but see it as a necessary evil. Ethics just *is* a complex and difficult study, they argue, and advancements in the understanding of it can come only through trained analysis of critical obscurities in carefully discriminated abstractions.

Whatever may be the merits of the motives which inspired this division of labor, a notable consequence of it has been the irrelevance of much of ethical theory to the ethical lives that people are actually striving to lead. The irrationalism that underlies much of contemporary normative discourse in the political domain and the mass media can be viewed as a fully understandable, if tragic, response to this unhealthy divorce between theory and practice. While the distinction between ethical theory and ethical practice is a venerable and valuable one, its entanglement with the modern professionalization of philosophy so that philosophy is only legitimately concerned with the former, has, I believe, been costly.

Many teachers who have perceived this irrelevance have sought to alleviate it by emphasizing 'practical ethics' and achieved some measure of success in probing problems such as abortion, euthanasia, and civil rights issues. But all too often this approach has meant either the purchase of relevance at the expense of theoretical depth and consistency or the engagement in increasingly implausible gymnastic attempts to reconnect principles to practice.

I suggest, instead, that the solution lies neither in making ethics less theoretical and more practical nor in elevating the functional separation of theory from practice into a professional creed, but rather in modifying what we take to be ethical theory so that it may operate more freely and more wisely in the domain of concrete ethical life. In particular, this will require that we dislodge the notion of principle from its current position of centrality in ethical theory.

Before we proceed, however, let us clarify the nature of the impasse to which we have been brought. The failure of ethical theory's preoccupation with principle is most clearly revealed in two contemporary problems faced by the project of ethical understanding—the well-known problem of moral relativism, and a variously named problem which I have called "the theoretician's dilemma."[5]

The Problem of Relativism

The problem of relativism, I believe, is one of two core problems defining the limits of the ethics of principle. It is not really one problem, but rather a syndrome of problems arising out of the failure to give a satisfactory account of the relationships between fact, rationality, and value. Moral relativism is the thesis that moral actions and attitudes cannot be evaluated by criteria of reason and value that have their source and criteria of legitimation outside the culture of that society.[6] It goes much further than the innocuous and obviously true remark that a substantial portion of our ethical thinking is shaped by, and applicable only within, the cultural meanings and social norms of the society that we inhabit. In its more radical form it implies that if the (majority of) persons in a society or sub-society believe that an action is the right thing for them to do, it follows a priori that it really is the right thing for them to do. While few people who claim to be moral realtivists endorse such a bald statement, they are usually at a loss to show why it is not a natural inference from the things that they do believe.

The problem of moral relativism has two aspects. It is a problem of authority (how can we judge between alternative accounts of the right if there is no universal authority to appeal to?) and a problem of discernment (how can we judge between alternative accounts of the right if they spring from different concrete visions of the good? These two aspects of the problem of relativism reveal a hidden bankruptcy in the separation between a theoretical study of formal principles and a practical knowledge of the problems of moral life. The problem of authority reveals that the rationality of thought about concrete cases is *only* rational if it is integrated into a broad understanding of what is good, and not otherwise. The problem of discernment reveals that the rationality of principle is only rational in thought about concrete cases, and not otherwise.

The temptation to engage in polemics over relativism can be abated by recognizing that there are healthy and unhealthy versions of it. Healthy relativisim is a natural product of our growing sensitivity to context. Seung has put the point elegantly:

> Recently, some critics have begun to behave as though our contextual abyss were a swamp of misfortune thay had fallen into by some unfortunate accident. But this contextual or hermeneutic abyss is not a gift of accident, but our own achievement, which has been secured through our gradual realization of contextual significance. It is not a cognitive chaos that has been thrown over our fumbling intellect by some evil genius, but an epistemic space that has been created by our maturing contextual awareness.[7]

Healthy relativities concern the moral, intellectual, and physical capacities of the agent. For example, it may be the moral responsibility of a strong and healthy male to physically interfere when a mugging is in progress, although a frail and senile elderly woman would have no such responsibility. Moral responsibility is also relative to circumstance as well. A doctor has the moral responsibility to treat someone in distress, but a child does not. Truth and morality are obviously relational concepts, so it is equally obvious that they have relativities. For example, truth is relative to both facts and discourse, and morality is relative to both the capacities of the agent and the circumstance he finds himself in.

Unhealthy relativism is unable to distinguish right from wrong, science from superstition, rational judgement from capricous belief. It insists that if a society, sub-society, or individual believes that an action is the right thing to do, then it really is the right thing to do it. The failings of moral relativism as a world-view are fairly easy to identify:

1. Moral relativism justifies intolerance as much as tolerance, since intolerant societies cannot be evaluated.
2. It entails that reformers are always wrong because they object to prevailing norms.
3. It makes morality solely a tool of power because power structures determine social norms, thereby removing the legitimation for both law and civil disobedience: it gives us no framework from which to judge how power should be used.
4. It relies on simplistic notions of both individual and society, ignoring the fact that no individual inherits the values of just one group and that there are many variously sourced voices within an individual.
5. It frequently implies a crude majoritarianism ("the majority is always right"), which clearly offends our intuitions about social justice to minorities.
6. It entails that we would not only have to refrain from evaluating the behavior of others (from corrupt politicians to Hitler), but we would be unable to evaluate our own behavior, other than to recognize that it is conforming or deviant: conscience would atrophy.

Given these failings, why would anyone want to embrace relativism? One reason is that many see it as the only alternative to a moribund principle-based ethics. Principle-based ethics locates the criteria of legitimation in an abstract domain, whereas cultural meanings and social norms inhabit a concrete domain. Despite valiant efforts by modern philosophy to establish connections between the two domains, their blank unlikeness makes the failure of legitimation and the problem of moral relativism inevitable. On such a model, ethics as the theory of right practice is an oxymoron: the prepositional 'of' has no reference. Not until the criteria of legitimation are anchored in a concrete understanding, one which recognizes its source in culture and history while acquiring the capacity to make authoritative judgements on that culture through a self-knowledge which carries its own warrant, will the problem of relativism be laid to rest.

Another reason is that, in popular rhetoric, moral relativism has become identified with the current political ideal of uncritical pluralism which has largely replaced (or lessened in importance) older ideals of commonweal, social order, and racial, tribal, or cultural identity. This laudable inclusiveness has consequences for social meaning which, once the rhetorical underbrush has been cleared away, are somewhat less than desirable. In a pluralistic society, for example, many find it difficult to draw the distinction between authority and democratically sanctioned brute force. Also, a pluralistic tolerance often masks an inability or unwillingness to face structurally entrenched failures in social planning. Different conceptions of what is right in particular cases often reveal large-scale differences in visions of social good. Without a method of discernment which can navigate these differences, a vicious loop of inactivity results in which the understanding of particular right awaits upon social norm, and social norm awaits upon understanding of particular right. The solution of diluting both individual ethical understanding and social norms to their lowest possible level has so far been shown to be of only limited value.

The Theoretician's Dilemma

Independent of the problems of authority and discernment implicit in the problem of relativism, a broader problem of application is inherent in principle-based ethics, a problem that has been often lamented but rarely clearly identified. I call this problem the theoreticians's dilemma, adapting a term from Carl Hempel. In a famous article on the philosophy of science, Hempel examined the problem of the purpose of theoretical terms in scientific explanation and prediction.[8] Theorizing seems to generate a paradox. The terms and principles of a scientific theory serve the purpose of establishing intelligible connections among observational phenomena. But if this is possible, then it must also be possible to dispense with such interpretive theoretical entities and replace them with laws linking observational antecedents directly to observational consequents. The theoretician thus seems caught in a classical dilemma:

If the terms and principles of a theory serve their purpose they are unnecessary, as just pointed out, and if they don't serve their purpose they are surely unnecessary. But given any theory, its terms and principles either serve their purpose or they don't. Hence, the terms and principles of any theory are unnecessary.[9]

In ethics, *because* it deals with practice rather than observation, the problem becomes more acute. When we attempt to bring abstract moral theory to bear on concrete ethical situations, we often find ourselves faced with a dilemma: the more precise and comprehensive our theory of the principles involved in concrete situations of choice and decision, and the more thorough our characterization of the reasons why these principles should be followed, the less relevant and applicable our theory becomes, both to the exigencies of the situation and to the actual motivations of the persons involved.

Concrete situations lack the clean lines of principle. They do not reveal of themselves the place or manner in which principles are to be applied, nor what form they are to take. How, then, are we to know how (or whether) a principle is to be applied in practice? Do we appeal to theory or to practice? If to theory, we seem quickly to arrive at a vicious regress: in order to apply a principle to practice we need to have a principle of application, but to know which principle of application to adopt in practice we need a further principle. And so on. Are we then to appeal to practice, as those who are fond of something they call "common sense" would recommend? But now we are faced with a dilemma. Practice is already theoretically informed, whether we are conscious of it or not. The ethical equivalent of scientific explanation is conscious reflection on how one's principles apply to one's current situation. Even those who believe that moral behavior is largely a matter of the exercise of good habits acquired via childhood conditioning would still, for the most part, be less than sanguine about abandoning their thought processes while they are engaged in actions—especially those actions which take a long time to complete, are ethically complex, and tend to recur.

Let's use the following example to illustrate this dilemma. Suppose a soldier fighting in Vietnam has been brought up to believe that it is wrong to kill another human being, but he also believes in a general sort of way that in some circumstances this principle may be abrogated. To what kind of thinking could he appeal for help in resolving his moral uncertainties in the context of his current situation? To gain concrete relevance he might decide to lower the level of abstraction of his principle and give it substantive form and qualification. For example, 'do not kill' might be modified to 'if you are a soldier fighting in the jungle do not kill your enemy unless not doing so involves reasonable risk of endangering a mission of reasonable importance or future mission of such importance.' Relevance is gained but at the cost of much of the original principle's universality and justificational authority. On the other hand, the soldier might make a theoretical choice to maintain the original principle and attempt to derive concrete guidance from it by purely formal procedures of inference. Adopting a radically pacifist stance, he would refuse to admit circumstances which might morally require him to kill. The universality and justificational authority of the principle would be maintained, but at the cost, presumably, of both immediate relevance and much of the concrete psychological appeal to interests which forms so large a part of our motivation to action. While some might applaud a pacifism-at-all-costs stance, it is difficult not to treat such a strategy as overly rigid formalism in other cases (as when the principle 'do not lie' is considered in the concrete situation of choosing how to answer the Gestapo officer who has asked you the location of your Jewish sister).

The theoretician's dilemma brings to light how principle-based ethics fails to unite principle, situation, and motivation in the required way. On the one hand, if the principle is given too much substantive content, it loses its universality and hence its ability to command our (theoretical) reason, insofar as this is guided by requirements of consistency and completeness. On the other hand, if it is given too little substantive content, it loses its intelligible threads of connection with concrete situations and hence its ability to command our (practical) will. A principle-based notion of moral understanding thus gives a significantly incomplete picture of the rationally integrated moral agent. If we fail to will *in concreto* the principle which our reason has determined to be right (the moral failing labeled weakness of the will) or fail to acknowledge as our own a desire which runs contrary to principle (the moral failing labeled self-deception), then such an ethic has few psychological resources to turn to other than the dubious comforts of self-accusation and repression. Yet the fault may sometimes lie not with ourselves but with our theory. I believe that the theoretician's dilemma is the *reductio ad absurdum* of the view that principles hold the key to moral understanding. Another touchstone must be sought.

These kinds of problems have usually led philosophers to invoke some other ability to explain how we make the transition from theory to practice—usually some version of the notion of 'practical reason.' A purely principle-based ethical theory such as Kant's treats investigation of the theory-practice relation as something which falls outside the scope of ethics proper (the investigation into the meaning and truth of moral principles) and relegates it to the domain of casuistry (the study of how and when principles are to be applied in practice).[10] As a consequence, practical reason itself (i.e., moral choice) necessarily remains opaque to reflective understanding. Utilitarianism, which is principle-based in its conception of the right but not of the good (this latter being apprehended by an irrational sympathy), permits a more intelligible but less moral conception of practical reason. The tradition which began with Bentham's hedonic calculus of pleasure and evolved into the complex inter-personal utility comparisons of contemporary decision theory became more and more transparent to critical judgment but less and less descriptive of the genuine operation of moral understanding in the practical realm. Kantian and utilitarian appeals to practical reason are therefore not *solutions* to the theoretician's dilemma, but a re-naming of their inability to explain the connection between intellibility and moral motivation.

Neither of these appeals to a practical reason, I believe, provides an adequate solution to the theoretician's dilemma. The Kantian notion is ultimately obscure and lacking an adequate moral psychology. To say, as Kant does, that practical reason is a reason that motivates the will, without providing an adequate psychology of that process, is unenlightening. The utilitarian notion of practical reason, while certainly not obscure (being simply a procedure for calculating maximal satisfaction of given values) leaves those values without a rational evaluation procedure of their own. And the utilitarian appeal to sympathy as a source of moral motivation, although it appeals to some as a healthy admission of the limits of theory, too easily turns into a comfortable agreement to stop thinking—which does not sound so comfortable when one considers how often such amiable ignorance so leads to apathy, aimlessness, and violence. The concept of sympathy simply places moral motivation in a black box within the psyche. Appeals to practice mean little if it is recognized that practice has only two options—to be enlightened by understanding or not to be so enlightened. The horns of the dilemma remain firm.

The revival of interest in virtue-based ethics over the last two decades has brought with it a more promising notion of 'practical judgement' deriving from Aristotle's concept of *phronesis*.[11] It is more promising because it is not principle-based. Aristotle distinguished the various domains toward which rational understanding directed itself according to the purpose for which such understanding was pursued. This was the basis for his distinctions between theoretical, practical, and productive understanding. Theoretical understanding (*theoria*, view or vision) was pursued for its own sake. Practical understanding (*praxis*, the speaking and acting together of human beings) was pursued for the sake of action. Productive understanding (*poiesis*, craft-skill) is pursued for the sake of making. (Making is distinguished from acting in that it pursues an end outside of itself).[12] Because action involved both rational and nonrational parts of the soul, the understanding appropriate to it could not achieve the excellence of the wholly rational part (*sophia*, theoretical wisdom), but only the excellence of the partly rational part (desire plus appetite), *phronesis* (practical wisdom or prudence). *Phronesis* is a 'deliberative desire' which at the same time discovers concrete ends as well as relates those ends to available means.[13] Yet Aristotle is notoriously silent about the details of the moral psychology of deliberative desire, and his reliance on a natural teleology of human ends to provide the test of *phronesis* places great strain on its relevance to a contemporary world which has abandoned the physics of final causality and become much more aware of the diversity of human goals. Part of the task of rehabilitating virtue ethics has been accomplished by Alasdair MacIntyre's relativization of virtue to practices in *After Virtue*. Virtues, for MacIntyre, are not excellences of the human species per se, but those character traits necessary for accomplishing the goods inherent in certain practices which have stood the test of time.

Another part of the task, I believe, is to provide the missing moral psychology and *that* will require a re-examination of Aristotle's overly narrow treatment of the imagination. (I shall return to this later.)

THE MARK OF THE ETHICAL

How necessary, really, is the notion of principle to the task of ethical understanding? Modern ethical theories have treated it as central, locating the mark of the ethical person in the degree to which he or she submits his or her will to a particular kind of rule. In the case of utilitarianism this is a substantive rule of benefit to persons in general, in the case of Kantian ethics it is a rule characterized by formal features of its manner of representation to the mind—namely, universality derived from the conception of law itself and categorical necessity derived from the recognition that it is addressed to a being possessed of a will (i.e., a being capable of acting according to its conception of a law). Moralities of principle provide, it is argued, an objective description of the ethical field. Concepts of right and wrong primarily apply to a certain kind or class of thing which can be captured by lawlike statements—namely actions. These are treated as part of the objective furniture of the universe in the sense of being logically independent of descriptions of the empirically experienced mind or self. Such a description leaves the thinking and experiencing subject out by design, thereby gaining purity, but at the cost of point.

The proposal offered in this book is that persons, rather than principles, should take center stage in our understanding of the ethical. We should not first seek to define the ethical through an Aristotelian 'division according to objects,' but seek a division according to subjects or persons. This does not mean that a person-based ethic abandons objective considerations, nor that it denies the importance of acting on principle. It does imply, however, that the abstract formulations of moral principle are incomplete at the level of our *understanding* of what constitutes right relations with other persons insofar as they are persons (not merely incomplete at the level of our ability to apply that understanding).

If we approach the ethical as, in essence, a feature of persons (rather than of kinds of actions or properties of principles), we find that we must look at ethical thought in a different way, since persons are not objects, or at least not objects in the usual sense of the term. Persons are representers of objects, subjective agents, and self-identifiers. They are also in an important sense processes rather than fixed entities (although they do possess some important long-term continuities such as character, personality, and self-concept). Persons straddle the domains of subjectivity and objectivity. Persons have ethical objects (e.g., principles), but they are not themselves ethical objects. Persons resist objectification.

An ethics of persons has to begin by acknowledging some of the force behind the problem of relativism and the theoretician's dilemma. Ethical objects may show significant variance from person to person, culture to culture, situation to situation. And inferences from principle often fail to be determinative of particular actions in concrete situations. Are we then to despair and say that there is no such thing as right relation between persons? Or that right relations are whatever an individual or a society thinks they are? Or that there are objective right relations, but they have no rationally compelling appeal to concrete individuals? I don't think so, but an adequate reply will, I believe, require some significant reconfiguration of our cartography of the ethical. In particular, it will require a *rapprochement* between moral philosophy and moral psychology (especially the psychology of the self), the detachment of the concept of ethical rationality from that of scientific rationality, and the development of concepts able to serve as bridges of intelligibility and motivation between theory and practice.

Such pessimism as is generated by the problem of relativism and the theoretician's dilemma about the ineffectiveness of theoretical understanding in ethics stems, I suggest, from an unnecessarily firm attachment to the paradigm of *theoria* as the contemplation of timeless truths. As such, it is detached from the active practical life of the ethical person, from the structure of concrete motivation of persons in particular situations. But the ends of theory and the ends of practice need not be placed in such dire opposition. It is possible to treat ethical thinking as an evolving, historically grounded, and psychologically structured activity without either denigrating it as irrational or replacing the category of theoretical understanding with a mysteriously primitive notion of practical understanding. We might call such thinking "concrete reflection" and use it to refer to the more concrete kind of thinking that we do when we are engaged, not so much in the abstractions of ethical theory, but in circumstances of concrete choice and attitude.

The ideal of rationality appropriate to such thinking would be that of a maximal comprehension of the motives for our actions. This comprehension would of necessity include as an essential component a dimension of self-understanding psychologically prior to the formation of principle. Such a reflection would include many of the standard elements of theorizing: inferring, analyzing, synthesizing, conjecturing, and interpreting. In addition, however, the self and its motivations will be seen to be caught up in these processes in a unique way. Certain distinctions common to ethical theorizing will be significantly absent— notably the categorical distinction between desire and obligation. When we derive a result (i.e., a choice or an attitude) in concrete moral reflection, we have not merely grasped that we ought to do something or believe something; we have determined that we want to do what we ought to do. Somewhere in our psyche, *is* and *ought* have coallesced. (Of course, a distinction could still be made between kinds or levels of desire, but this is no longer the categorical distinction defining the moral as it is in Kant's distinction between inclination and will.)

The concept of rational self-understanding invoked by such an ethic will need to include an account of how moral representations enter the self's dynamics of desire without loss of content, authority, or intelligibility. It is to this question that the theory of imaginative idealization is addressed. For it is through imaginative idealization that individuals come to make the foundational (although not necessarily unalterable) distinctions which constitute the structure of both their ethical interpretations and their ethical motivations. Ideals are envisionings of the self's good life, and they are products of imagination rather than the apprehension of the truth of principles. To say that our ethical desires are an imaginative product does not, however, cut them off from reality or rational scrutiny. By the end of this book I hope to have shown that imagination may also possess a genuinely theoretical role in the synthetic apprehension of ethical unities, and not merely the heuristic one of applying theory to concrete cases.

IMAGINATION'S FATE

Philosophers have tended to neglect the concept of imagination as a means of understanding the domain of the ethical. One reason for this has no doubt been the variety of conceptions of the imagination which have been developed over the centuries. The imagination is a notoriously difficult concept to define. A study of its history reveals a complex web of conflicting meanings and distinctions. It is abundantly evident that the English word 'imagination' (as well as its other-language equivalents) has been used to refer to a multitude of distinct notions.[14] Even when a subset of more or less congruent meanings have been isolated, the concept has rarely been advanced beyond the typological level to that of genuine theory. And despite a contemporary revival of interest in the topic, it remains an essentially contested concept: no generally acceptable theory even of the main subsets of the concept of the imagination is presently available.

In ethics generally, the imagination has usually been discussed in the context of practical or applied ethics. Theoretical accounts of what it is about actions and persons that make them either ethical or unethical have tended to minimize the role of the imagination or pass over it altogether. This is clearly the case in Kantian ethics (see Chapter 3). Although Kant assigns an important if obscure place to imagination in theoretical understanding, he largely restricts its place in morals to the practical business of moral judgment (the application of principle to cases). Utilitarianism does indeed assign a much more prominent place to imagination, especially to sympathy theories of ethics deriving from the work of Hume and Adam Smith, but the question of whether this is a mode of understanding or a heuristic device is unclear (see Chapter 2).

Despite vigorous attempts by theoreticians, the concept of imagination has been difficult to dislodge. It plays too large a role in too many areas of human life to be easily banished to the realm of mere heuristics. Philosophers have conveniently passed the elaboration of the imagination over to poetry and literature, thereby providing this vital, if awkward, concept something of a home. This has been a joint program of thinkers who in their philosophical conclusions are often otherwise fiercely opposed. On the one hand, romantics and neo-romantics (such as Dilthey, Schleiermacher, Croce, Begson, and Collingwood) have encouraged the migration in the conviction that truth is made rather than discovered, and the poetic imagination is the ideal vehicle for this making.[15] On the other hand, positivists and neo-positivists, convinced that imagination has nothing to do with truth, have relegated imaginative thought to the 'emotive' realms of poetry and art in an effort to wash their hands of it once and for all. Again, from a rather different direction, critical theorists such as

Habermas and Apel, recognizing that imagination has a cognitive role as creative insight, tend to invoke literary models of understanding as opposed to formal (or 'conceptual,' or 'technical,' or 'instrumental,' or 'calculative'—the phrase varies with one's polemical target) models. In each model, moral judgement and sympathy pass beyond the pale of theoretical understanding into some form of social praxis.

The reason imagination seems to so many to be a literary-poetic activity, however, is that it is posed in opposition to a Platonic view of knowledge as the conceptual understanding of a reality possessed of form independent of the consciousness that apprehends it. According to this view, imagination is regarded as offering, at best, the bittersweet illusion of reality. This view, regarded by many today as rather old-fashioned, has its ancestry in Plato's depiction of the philosopher's journey as the escape from semblance toward true being:

> Such is the life of the gods; but of other souls, that which follows God best and is likest to him lifts the head of the charioteer into the outer world, and is carried round in the revolution, troubled indeed by the steeds, and with difficulty beholding true being; while another only rises and falls, and sees, and again fails to see by reason of the unruliness of the steeds. The rest of the souls are also longing after the upper world and they all follow, but not being strong enough they are carried round below the surface, plunging, treading on one another, each striving to be first; and there is confusion and perspiration and the extremity of effort; and many of them are lamed or have their wings broken through the ill-driving of the charioteers; and all of them after a fruitless toil, not having attained to the mysteries of true being, go away, and feed upon opinion [semblance].[16]

The delightfully bewitching images and metaphors of literature and poetry ought certainly to be cultivated, it is believed, not because they advance our understanding of what is real or right or good, but because of certain socially salutary effects on the habits of mind of the person so bewitched. This plea for a truce between philosophical truth and an essentially irrational imagination in a war which has been consciously fought since Plato, has received elegant statement in the work of P. F. Strawson:

> The region of the ethical, then, is a region of diverse, certainly incompatible and possibly practically conflicting ideal images or

pictures of a human life, or of human life; and it is a region in which many such incompatible pictures may secure at least the imaginative, though doubtless not often the practical, allegiance of a single person. Moreover this statement itself may be seen not merely as a description of what is the case, but as a positive evaluation of evaluative diversity. Any diminution in this variety would impoverish the human scene. The multiplicity of conflicting pictures is itself the essential element in one of one's pictures of man.[17]

The difficulties in applying universal principles amid the diverse concrete apprehensions of our world have also been well charted by Stuart Hampshire:

> There are two faces of morality: the rational and articulate side and the less than rational, the historically conditioned, fiercely individual, imaginative, parochial, the less than fully articulate, side.[18]

And:

> Moral conflicts are of their nature inelimanable. . . . The worth and value of a person's life and character, and also of a social structure, are always undetermined by purely rational considerations.[19]

Just as the pluralistic clash of value systems is inevitable and rationally unresolvable, so too must be the work of the literary-poetic imagination as it performs its task:

> I am suggesting that it is the nature of imagination that it generally deals in conflicts and contradictions, in dubious meanings, and not in definite conclusions and in unambiguous assertions. The energy in any imaginative work comes from that destruction of single-mindedness which allows different interpretations at different levels. This ambiguity, and this absence of reliable tendency, was a principle ground of Plato's banishment of the poets and of his plea for censorship; this, and the fact that the imagination of the poet, musician, or painter plays upon the surface of things, and is unconcerned with their underlying rational structure.[20]

There is much that is sound in this position, particularly the call for tolerance, moral exploration, and the recognition that loyalties and commitments may sometimes be quite justifiably rooted in purely historical circumstances rather than in reverence for a principle. But I think that it is ultimately mistaken. A truce arrived at in this way between imagination and reason, particularly in the domain of ethics, will not be adequate to either our theoretical or our practical interests. A separationist peace attained by limiting the work of imagination to the literary side of a literary understanding/philosophical understanding dichotomy will be as temporary as one obtained by placing the imagination on the practical side of a practical understanding/theoretical understanding dichotomy.[21] For one thing, it obscures the nonfictive capacities of the imagination. Literary understanding is capable of addressing and instructing our ethical perplexities in a fully cognitive manner. A novel or a poem can inspire our mind as well as our hearts.[22] Further, this pluralist emphasis on the imagination's ability to dislodge encrusted categorizations is only half the story. The other half is the constructive ability of the imagination to dispel illusory distinctions and differences, to discover new synthetic unities, and to rediscover old ones.

For philosophers to pass the concept of imagination over to poetry and literature is a premature abandonment of responsibility. We have been persuaded to do so because of a meta-philosophical difficulty generated by a principle-based conception of rationality. Namely, if philosophy is theoretical understanding, and if to understand something theoretically is to explicate the principles of its operation, and if imagination does not proceed according to explicated principles, then imagination and philosophy have finally nothing to do with each other. We find it difficult not to agree with Samuel Johnson's characterization of it as a "licentious and vagrant faculty." But the responsibility of evolving theory is to monitor its relation to practice. It would indeed be an arrogance of theory to attempt to explicate, in a practically reproducible way, the principles of operation of a process such as the imagination which is essentially nonreproducible. Nevertheless, although the activity of the imagination may be beyond the reach of theory in the sense of being replaceable by it, the relation of the concept 'imagination' to our other moral concepts is a legitimate and viable theoretical concern. It is an equal arrogance of practice to assume that an explicated concept of imagination cannot aid it. Such arrogance stems from the same radical divorce of theory and practice which has produced the ivory tower so much lamented today.

It is true that the attempt to disestablish the philosophical concept of an ethical imagination by placing all consideration of it within the literature side of the philosophy/literature opposition *does* grant the imagination a quasi-ethical role, even in the form of an ethically neutral literary-poetic activity. In practice, it may have the positive ethical benefits of expanding one's moral horizons and perhaps of influencing one's character development in a salutary if subrational way.[23] But this fails to answer (except by saying that no answer is possible) the urgent questions which theoretical ethics must address if it is to continue as a legitimate form of human inquiry. The limits of tolerance are left undefined; the purely poetic concept of imagination fails to distinguish between ethical and unethical ideals and commitments, the problem of relativism remains entrenched (particularly as a pedagogical problem); and the connection between theoretical understanding and concrete motivation is again left unexplained.

CHAPTER 2

Hume and Smith: Imagination in the Extension of Sympathy

A man, to be greatly good, must imagine intensely and comprehensively; he must put himself in the place of another and of many others; the pains and pleasures of his species must become his own. The great instrument of moral good is the imagination; and poetry administers to the effect by acting upon the cause.

Percy Bysshe Shelley[1]

Before turning to imagination's role in ethical idealization, we will examine two other areas of ethical life in which imagination also plays a significant role: the extension of sympathy (the adoption of the point of view of others in their pleasures and pains), and moral judgment (traditionally understood as the application of moral principles to particular cases). Each of these areas has a history of discussion behind them. But in neither case has an adequate place in theory been found for the imagination as a mark of the ethical person. In both cases, imagination's role has traditionally been thought to be practical rather than theoretical, a matter of skill or experience rather than articulate understanding, a heuristic aid in applying ethical principles or motivating us to them, rather than of discovering what it is about certain relations with others that makes them ethical.

This may, perhaps, be considered appropriate in the case of moral judgment. Under an ethic of principles the practical side of ethics is limited to application (moral judgment) and motivation. Whatever theoretical content the theory-practice relationship does have, can be treated separately from ethics proper under the rubric of casuistry. Some might argue that no special ethical imagination is required for the application of principles: in imagining how a moral principle might apply in practice, no particular *kind* of imagination (i.e., an ethical kind) is required.[2] This does not seem to be fully convincing. Although a broad imaginative facility may be of some use here, it remains necessary to select the aspects of a situation to be attended to. Without an imagination specifically devoted to seeking out ethically significant aspects (i.e., one that was ethical in its psychological origins rather than simply in the objects of its attention), ethical discernment would flounder, particularly in complex cases.

In discussions of sympathy it is more readily agreed that the imagination is a means by which we come to know morally relevant aspects. But it is difficult to say what is specifically ethical (in contrast, say, to aesthetic, cognitive, or emotional) about the imagination's work here. Kant regards sympathy as ethically irrelevant, and utilitarians treat is as either a more or less efficient method of data gathering, or as a useful but morally neutral psychological prompt to moral behavior (the right being measured by consequences rather than intentions).

The imagination's role in the extension of sympathy to others has received considerable attention by moral philosophers. There has been a long history of discussion, from the sympathy-based ethics of Hume and Adam Smith to contemporary utilitarian investigations of the epistemic warrant provided by sympathy in interpersonal utility comparisons.[3] The eighteenth-century interest in moral imagination focused on its role in sympathy, and the chief interest in sympathy was its role in the production of moral sentiments. For Hume and Smith, this took the form of a moral philosophy which was not so much interested in the prescriptive question of why we should be moral as in the descriptive question of how we come to have moral sentiments. For Hume, "moral distinctions depend entirely on certain peculiar sentiments of pain and pleasure, and . . . whatever mental quality in ourselves or others gives us a satisfaction, by the survey or reflexion, is of course virtuous; as everything of this nature, that gives uneasiness, is vicious."[4] The centrality of sympathy in the origin of moral sentiments stems from its being the vehicle by which we enter into the sentiments of others: "Our fancy easily changes its situation; and either surveying ourselves as we appear to others, or considering others as they feel themselves, we enter, by that means, into sentiments which no way belong to us, and in which nothing but sympathy is able to interest us."[5] Behind this was Hume's assumption of a community of human nature: "The minds of all men are similar in their feelings and operations, nor can anyone be actuated by any affection, of which all others are not, in some degree, susceptible."[6] This community, added to Hume's conviction that a major task of moral philosophy was to account for the transition of the passions, led him to declare: "Sympathy interests us in the good of mankind. . . . "[7]

Although they share common starting points, Hume and Smith explicate the moral psychology of sympathy in significantly different fashion. Both see its primary vehicle to be the imagination, and both couch their views within the associationist presuppositions of their time. For Hume, "sympathy . . . is nothing but the conversion of an idea into an impression by the force of the imagination."[8] For Smith,

> Though our brother is upon the rack . . . it is by the imagination only that we can form any conception of what are his sensations. Neither can that faculty help us to this any other way, than by representing to us what would be our own, if we were in his case. It is the impressions of our own sense only, not those of his, which our imaginations copy. By the imagination we place ourselves in his situation . . . we enter as it were into his body, and become in some measure the same person with him.[9]

But, whereas Hume views the conative force of the imagination as primarily channeled through the emotions or passions—

> Wherever our ideas of good and evil acquire a new vivacity the passions become more violent and keep pace with the imagination in all its variations . . . [10]

—Smith posits a more complex psychology in which sympathy requires, in some sense, a transfer of self or person:

> When I condole with you for the loss of your only son, in order to enter into your grief . . . I do not only change circumstances with you, but I change persons and characters.[11]

Although Smith's account is more interesting, it is also more obscure. Is the transfer of person a literal accomplishment or only a metaphor? If the former, much more theory is required than Smith provides concerning the structure of the self and the mechanism of transfer. If the latter (as his "as it were" implies), then it must be acknowledged that Smith's account is a philosophical placeholder only, pointing to an interesting set of questions but awaiting replacement by critically transparent argument. Unexplicated metaphors, whatever their place in life and the movement of thought, can have no lasting place in the body of philosophical knowledge.

Even if some of the key movements of the psychological operation of sympathy could be specified,[12] any sympathy-based theory of ethics must eventually face a crucial question: What is it about imaginative sympathy, or a certain kind of imaginative sympathy, which marks it as specifically ethical? In considering this question we need to be sensitive to the fact that it calls for two levels of analysis. On the one hand, it asks for a feature or features of sympathy which makes it intelligibly recognizable as an ethical ability. On the other hand, it asks for a specification of the ethical in general in such a way that sympathy might be able to lay some rational claim over our active desire.

Lacking a theory of the structure of imagination (a lack of which they were acutely aware),[13] the eighteenth-century sympathy theorists split the answer to this question in a way that has had major repercussions today. The feature that marked the mental act of sympathy as ethical was the kind of object that sympathy was directed toward—the welfare (in particular, the happiness) of other persons. And what marked sympathy as worthy of being acted upon, its ethicality in general, was the rational warrant derivable from the analytic device of the impartial or disinterested spectator. The ethical was defined by the sympathy that the ideal observer would feel, possessed of all the relevant facts and unbiased by personal interest.[14]

This produced an unfortunate result for moral philosophy, in the form of a growing theoretical gap between motivation and justification. From the motivational side, it could not fail to be realized that our sympathies and those of the ideal observer often differ. And to say that one simply ought to have ideal sympathies, or *ought* to strive to have them, is at best a cumbersome locution and at worst a dangerous piece of moral pedagogy fraught with psychological pitfalls. Telling a child who at a certain stage in his moral development is incapable of abstract sympathies that he *ought* to sympathize with the starving peasants of China—and that it is wrong of him not to have these sympathies—may easily lead to his having unnecessary feelings of guilt or to adopt pseudo-sympathies to placate his moralizing parents. And if in later life he is unable to distinguish genuine from pseudo-sympathy, we should not be surprised. It is far better to strive to cultivate his imagination in a non-enforcing way and with full respect for the appropriateness of his sympathies to his circumstances (if in fact they are appropriate) as our sympathies are appropriate to our circumstances (if in fact they are). Of course, his sympathies are less mature than ours. But the point is that this judgment is properly made not by referring our concrete sympathies to the abstraction of an ideal observer, but through our reflective understanding of the mental processes involved in each case and our sense of what is left out of the child's reflections.

From the justificational side, the prescriptions of the impartial spectator either possess rational legitimation independently of particular acts of sympathy or they do not.[15] That is, ideal sympathies either make no claim to be logically derived from actual sympathies, or actual sympathies are included as part of the justification. If they claim explanatory independence, motivational links still need to be established between that legitimation process and the interests and concerns of concrete individuals.[16] If they do not, if the impartial spectator is thought of as an averaging of sympathetic reactions or as a representative of certain ongoing social processes, the normative authority of such a device over individuals who lack those sympathies or who find themselves alienated by those social processes becomes difficult to discern.

Sympathy ethics is an attempt at an explanatory account of the origins of moral motivation. It does not provide a prescriptive analysis. It can be argued against both Hume and Smith that this is a failing: they do not separate moral virtues from general virtues of character such as good manners and prudence in financial matters. If one accepts the deontological intuition that there is such a distinction, that the psychological representations under which certain actions are performed discloses a unique moral "oughtness" that cannot be understood by a naturalistic tale of the origins of moral sentiments, then a more sophisticated moral psychology is required.

The moral psychology of sympathy has yet to be described adequately even in contemporary psychoanalytic language, and it is a large task. Certainly it can be distinguished from what Max Scheler[17] has called "emotional infection" (being swept up into the emotions of others), "community of feeling" (as when two parents "share" the sorrow of their child's death), and "emotional identification" (feelings following the identification of self with another). But to say, as Adam Smith does, that sympathy involves a "transfer of persons" would be going too far. The motivation comes from—and remains interior to—the concrete individual self, with the difference that it is not directed to the concrete self as in self-interest. Yet the depth psychology of this transfer has so far been left largely at the level of metaphor.

Certainly we can specify some broad criteria for a specifically ethical sympathy. First, the other's suffering would need to be felt in such a way that one is motivated to act to alleviate that suffering. Feelings of sorrow that do not lead to action may have aesthetic or other values, but they are not genuine sympathy in an ethical sense. Second, we would probably want to say that the pain at another's suffering should be mediated by a self-conscious reflection on the relation between that suffering and one's own good life. This reflection is subject to degrees, its terms may vary from language to language and culture to culture, and it may never emerge as articulated thought. But it must be present if the feeling is to be called an ethical one. One could construct hypothetical cases where a person has been hypnotized to feel pain at another's suffering and acts to alleviate that suffering, but we would be reluctant to call such feeling ethical specifically because conscious self-reflection is absent.

Yet these criteria would be insufficient if we do not also ask that persons articulate the rational ground of their sympathy to themselves. Might they not be deceiving themselves or us? How do we *know* that their feelings are ethical (or, for that matter, that our own are)? Perhaps, in the case of others, we can't know if they cannot articulate the reasons, although we might in some cases be able to make reasonable estimates. But this is not necessarily a failure of ethicality on their part. Rather it may be a limitation on the scope of public rationality. In our own case, if we are prompted by a feeling to alleviate a suffering, and sense (rather than articulate to ourselves) that that suffering is soundly connected to the realization of our good life, then we can say neither that we know nor that we do not know. We have reached a juncture between public, articulate rationality and private rationality in which imagination takes a more active role. We are not sure. But because it is our self that is concerned, rather than another whose domain of autonomy must be respected (even in some cases where we can be *almost* certain that they are lying or deceiving themselves), we can be much more rigorous in our demands. At such a juncture, our imagination and our drive for articulate thought may be called upon to make a new synthesis.

Ethical action requires reflective consciousness in which motivation and justification at some point meet. Partially embedded as it is in the category of spontaneous feeling, sympathetic imagination (i.e., representing to oneself in an affectively vivid way what it feels like to be another) is of itself neither a psychologically compelling nor a rationally authoritative motive to morality. Pictures of starving children shown during a telethon may lead many to shed sympathetic tears, but comparatively few people take any action. Indeed, some people regard their tears as sufficient discharge of their responsibility.

Certainly we may agree with Shelley that sympathetic imagination fosters ethical consciousness. But (as many have found) the attempt to take this to the point of *grounding* the ethical in sympathy has only led to the further separation of ethical theory and ethical practice—with imagination firmly restricted to the realm of practice. That such a divorce was dangerous is evident in Kant's artificial and ad hoc attempt to recover for ethical thought an 'obligation' to sympathy within the notion of practical reason:

> Now humanity can be located either in the *power* and *will* to *share* in others' *feelings* (*humanitas practica*) or merely in the *susceptibility*, given by nature itself, to feel joy and sadness in common with others (*humanitas aesthetica*). The first is *free*, and for this reason it is called a *partaking* (*communio sentiendi liberalis*); it is based on practical reason. The second is *unfree* (*communio sentiendi illiberalis, servillis*); like the communication of warmth or contagious diseases it can be called an *imparting* and also a suffering with another, since it spreads by natural means among men living near one another. It is only to *humanitas practica* that there is an obligation.[18]

This is surely bad psychology. The notion of a will to sympathy is a category mistake: will and feeling cannot be united by philosophical fiat. Certainly there is a difference between an educated sensibility and an unreflective one, even a difference between an active and a passive sympathy, but this difference is cultivated by more delicate mental avenues than the will to sympathize.

CHAPTER 3

Kant

Imagination runs riot when, in the still of the night, we study by
lamplight, or quarrel with imaginary opponents, or wander about
our room building castles in the air. . . . So the rule of curbing our
imagination by going to sleep early is a very useful rule of a
psychological regimen. But women and hypochondriacs (whose
trouble usually comes from this very habit) prefer the opposite
course.

Immanuel Kant, *Anthropology*[1]

KANT'S GENERAL THEORY OF THE IMAGINATION

Extracting a unified theory of imagination from Kant's writings is
difficult. Not only is he especially obscure on the subject, but his
ideas on it differ markedly from the first to the second editions of
the *Critique of Pure Reason*, the *Critique of Judgement*, and his
more popular writings.[2] Kant describes two somewhat different
faculties of imagination, one of which he calls *Einbildungskraft*,
and the other of which he calls *Phantasie*. Unfortunately, both of
these are often translated as 'imagination' in English. The latter is
the imaginative power of the artist, limited to aesthetic productions and to works of genius. The former is a broad epistemological power of representation, treated in detail in the first *Critique*:

> What is first given to us is appearance. When combined with
> consciousness it is called perception. . . . Now, since every
> appearance contains a manifold, and since different perceptions
> therefore occur in the mind separately and singly, a combination
> of them, such as they cannot have in sense itself, is demanded.
> There must therefore exist in us an active faculty for the synthe-
> sis of the manifold. To this faculty I give the title, imagination.[3]

A further complication is that Kant distinguishes two separate
kinds of *Einbildungskraft*, empirical and transcendental. The
empirical imagination is essentially reproductive. It reproduces

and connects sensory experience in the mind to form a comprehensive understanding of reality:

> As a power of [producing] intuitions even when the object is not
> present, imagination (*facultas imaginadi*) is either *productive* or
> *reproductive*—that is, either a power of exhibiting an object
> originally and so prior to experience (*exhibitio originaria*), or a
> power of exhibiting it in a derivative way, by bringing back to
> mind an empirical intuition we have previously had (*exhibitio
> derivata*). Pure intuitions of space and time are original exhibi-
> tions: all others presuppose empirical intuition which, when it is
> connected with the concept of the object so that it becomes
> empirical knowledge, is called *experience*. In so far as imagina-
> tion also produces images involuntarily, it is called *fantasy*. One
> who habitually mistakes such images for (inner or outer) experi-
> ence is *visionary*. The involuntary play of imagination in *sleep*
> (a healthy state) is called *dreaming*.[4]

In his treatment of the empirical imagination, Kant follows
the associationist psychology of his time, treating it as a matter of
fitting representations together from the ground up. This was
developed in the first edition of the *Critique of Pure Reason*. In
the second edition, Kant develops the transcendental function of
imagination, which has a much more productive role in representation.

Imagination in its pure or transcendental function *imposes* an
order on experience with the aid of certain logical rules and the a
priori rules of space and time. Kant sometimes called this the
"productive" imagination. Engell has argued that, in his early use
of the concept of the productive imagination, Kant meant something like the mind's ability to apprehend concepts which explain
experience, transfer them to a code such as mathematics or language, which is then used to order the experience.[5] This is the
kind of imagination needed, for instance, to imagine a line
extended infinitely in space.

We can distinguish four major stages in the development of
Kant's notion of imagination, all of which strive to account for
how the mind brings various representations into a unified judgment.[6]

Reproductive imagination.   Reproductive imagination provides
a synthesis of perceptual experience. It is the second element in
the synthesis of determinate judgment. A synthesis is "the act of

putting different representations together, and of grasping what is manifold in them in one act of knowledge."[7] Synthesis of apprehension in intuition organizes separate representations into a single image; synthesis of reproduction in imagination enables us to experience an object over time by synthesizing the object with previous representations; synthesis of recognition in a concept organizes the object into an object of a certain kind, as determined by a concept (a concept is a rule for structuring perceptual representations in a definite way).[8]

Productive imagination.　The productive imagination lifts the synthesis out of the realm of subjective psychological principles of association. This is imagination in its transcendental function. The fact that experience appears to us as *our* experience means that, in the synthesizing activity, we must presuppose the transcendental unity of consciousness (B 138). The imagination's work here is transcendental because it is given by the structure of consciousness as such. It is this transcendental function which makes it possible to experience public objects.

Productive imagination in its schematizing function.　This is Kant's attempt to link the empirical and transcendental functions of the imagination, which he develops in the section on the schematism of the understanding in the *Critique of Pure Reason*. In the case of empirical concepts, the schematism links the structure of consciousness to sensible intuitions. In the case of pure concepts of the understanding (the categories—causality, limitation, plurality, unity, etc.), the schematism links the structure of consciousness to the structure of objects as such. It is the latter, the imagination in its function in the transcendental schematism of the pure concepts of the understanding, which provides the necessary link between the material of sense and the formal structure of consciousness:

> Obviously there must be some third thing, which is homogeneous on the one hand with the category, and on the other hand with appearance, and which thus makes the application of the former to the latter possible. This mediating representation must be pure, that is void of all empirical content, and yet at the same time, while it must in one respect be *intellectual*, it must in another be *sensible*, such a representation is the *transcendental schema*.[9]

The creative imagination. In the *Critique of Judgement*, Kant tried to explain the imagination's role in judgments which were not determinate, but reflective and capable of producing new meanings. Judgments of taste are Kant's prime example of reflective judgment; they involve a free play of the imagination and our understanding. Reflective judgment is not purposeless, nor does it have the purposiveness which would be provided if it were operating according to a definite concept. There is a "purposiveness without any definite purpose," a *zweckmassigkeit*, a gathering toward an end which is attuned to the inner finalities of the objects (as revealed by their aspects) with which it deals. The result is a certain kind of cognitive harmony. Kant's theory of the creative imagination duplicates the distinction between the empirical and transcendental uses of the productive imagination through the concepts of the beautiful and the sublime. In both cases, pleasure is taken in our ability to make sense out of chaos (finality without a natural end) through this "harmonious interplay of understanding and imagination." Creative imagination is both productive *and* free.

In the case of objects judged to be beautiful, we apprehend the finality in the form of a sensuous image. When exemplified in human beings, such an image can be an expression of morality.[10] The aesthetic and the moral both take part in the ideal of beauty, which determines the one kind of object whose beauty compels universal assent. Such an object is man. White interprets Kant's difficult argument on this point as follows:

> Man and only man is that type of object which "has in itself the end (*Zweck*) of its real existence." Since man and man alone can "determine his ends by reason" man becomes the sole source constituting the archetype of taste. No other type of being displays its end such that it may be determined by reason. And since the realm of morality depends on the dictates of reason, a human being can appreciate the relation between beauty and morality more adequately when judging the beauty of another human being than when judging the beauty of another type of object. For Kant, morality depends on ends derived from reason, and beauty depends, in part, on the appearance of purposiveness without purpose. Thus, when the aesthetic perceiver connects human beauty with the purposive moral ends of the being judged beautiful, the perceiver enters into, and pleasurably enhances his awareness of his own nature as a moral being capable of appreciating beauty within a moral dimension.[11]

In our apprehension of the sublime, however, no such image is possible. We are thrown back from the object to our own powers. The object "lends itself to the presentation of a sublimity discoverable in the mind."[12] What the imagination leads us to are the ideas of reason. According to Warnock's[13] interpretation, what we stand in awe of is the fact that we are able to form such ideas.

Some aspects of Kant's fourth kind of imagination can be integrated with the notion of ethical idealization developed here. According to Kant, "beauty is the symbol of the morally good."[14] In aesthetic judgments of beauty, some worldly expression is given to the "inner finality of nature" through imagery. This enables the enlistment of feeling in moral interest. According to Mish'alani: "the abstract wrongness of an action must be mapped on to images of contamination and filth in order to enlist the services of sensibility for moral life and thus cultivate moral feeling."[15] But Kant is quite clear that such imagination is divorced from the understanding:

> All *hypotyposis* (presentation), *subjectio sub adspectum*, or sensible illustration, is twofold. It is either *schematical*, when to a concept comprehended by the understanding the corresponding intuition is given, or it is *symbolical*. In the latter case, to a concept only thinkable by reason, to which no sensible intuition can be adequate, an intuition is supplied with which is supplied a procedure of the judgement analogous to what it observes in schematism, i.e. merely analogous to the rule of this procedure, not to the intuition itself, consequently to the form of reflection merely and not to its content.[16]

Imagination in its creative sense performs a heuristic function leading the subject to the universal yet uncognizable supersensible ground of morality. Kant will allow this heuristic function to the imagination in morality, but he does not permit it to play a part in the transformative and cognitive self-awareness which a more psychoanalytic treatment of the imagination makes possible (see Chapter 4).

Kant's broader notion of the productive imagination is fraught with difficulties of interpretation, a full investigation of which lies outside the scope of this work. The productive imagination per se is essentially linked to the notion of transcendental categories, a concept which has obscurities of its own. The pure concepts are the preconditions of objectivity as such. The question naturally arises of how they do this in the schematism without producing an image object? According to Woods, it proceeds via "the production of an horizon within which objects can be comprehended."[17] Kant attempts to capture this operation of the transcendental imagination under the single concept of time, and the horizon is essentially a matter of ordering objects in temporal succession according to various rules. Thus the schema of the pure concept of magnitude is number, representing the process of successive addition in time. The schema of the pure concept of reality is something insofar as it fills time. The schema of substance is permanence of the real in time. The schema of causality is necessary succession in time. The schema of possibility is representation of a thing at some time or other:

> The schemata are thus nothing but *a priori* determinations of time in accordance with rules. . . . It is evident, therefore, that what the schematism of understanding effects by means of the transcendental synthesis of imagination is simply the unity of all the manifold of intuition in inner sense, and so indirectly the unity of apperception which as a function corresponds to the receptivity of inner sense. The schemata of the pure concepts of the understanding are thus the true and sole conditions under which these concepts obtain relation to objects and so possess *significance*. (A145–6)

The dense and forbidding explanatory minimalism of this reduction to temporal succession is further complicated by Kant's shift between representational and structural interpretations of the schematism. As a cognitive structure (i.e., a procedure), Kant's schematism is similar to the seeing-as model developed in the next chapter. But in his effort to tie it to the pure concepts of the understanding, Kant seems to treat it also as a conceptual product:

> The schema is in itself always a product of the imagination . . . the schema has to be distinguished from the image. . . . For with such a number as a thousand the image can hardly be surveyed and compared with the concept. This representation of a universal procedure of imagination in providing an image for a concept, I entitle the schema of this concept. Indeed it is schemata, not images of objects, which underlie our pure sensible concepts. . . . This schematism of our understanding, in its application to appearances and their mere form, is an art concealed in the depths of the human soul, whose real modes of activity nature is hardly likely ever to allow us to discover, and to have open to our gaze.[18]

Having located the schematism "in the depths of the human soul," further analysis of it is abrogated, and its linkage to concepts less transcendental than the categories is left uncharted. The characterization of the productive imagination as both sensible and intellectual is particularly obscure. Part of the problem, I think, is that the concept of the productive imagination is just too broad to explain by itself the multitude of coding strategies involved in the representation of experience.[19]

It is true, of course, that the concept developed here of the schematism is also broad. I would wish to expand the epistemological notion of *Einbildungskraft* to include syntheses not just of sensory contents, but also of contents that have already been synthesized. For example, when one enters a room one synthesizes the relationships between the people in the room. This assumes that visual syntheses have already been performed. The attunement to aspects can be continued across ever-increasing levels of interpretive complexity. Also, the notion of the schematism developed in Chapters 4 and 5 is not limited to providing an image for a content but includes a procedure for interpreting situations in ways that are original to the self. But the theoretical breadth is of a different order, a breadth of application rather than definiton. It permits of explication by empirical psychology, which is the concern of the next two chapters.

IMAGINATION IN MORAL JUDGMENT AND FEELING

As traditionally understood, moral judgment operates in the domain of the application of moral rules to particular cases. While some moral rules call for little exercise of judgment (e.g. Kant's "perfect duties," such as telling the truth), others call for a good deal of judgment (e.g., Kant's "imperfect duties," such as being generous). As Larmore notes, it is in the latter that we say the imagination comes into play:

> Moral imagination is our ability to elaborate and appraise different courses of action which are only partially determined by the given content of moral rules, in order to learn what in a particular situation is indeed the morally best thing to do. Moral imagination thus provides far greater evidence of an intrinsic interest in what is morally right than does merely the observance of moral rules.[20]

But how exactly does the imagination come into play here? This is a question which, for Kant, belongs to the anthropology of morals rather than the metaphysics of morals. Kant does not regard moral judgment as a significantly autonomous domain of theoretical understanding, for "understanding is the power of rules, and judgment the power of discovering the particular insofar as it is an instance of the rules."[21] A "right understanding" is "one that, by the *adequacy* of its concepts for knowledge of an object, is able and ready to apprehend *truth*."[22] This is ultimately possible for Kant because "the power of concepts contains the *universal* element of ideas."[23]

Broadly speaking, we might say that, for Kant, imagination's role in our understanding of our world is restricted to the synthesis of the sensible manifold (where it has both a productive and a reproductive function). Moral judgment and judgments of taste—not being matters of understanding through universal concepts, but of "applications"—are removed from the realm of theory to that of practice. To be sure, we could in principle always provide the rules linking our universal concepts with concrete cases. Hence, in theory imagination is not required for ethical *discovery*. But in practice (a) concrete cases are infinitely varied in character, making a theoretical predetermination of the linkages impossible, and (b) the intellectual limitations of human beings make other ways of proceeding desirable in practice.

> But ethics, because of the *play-room* it allows in its imperfect duties, inevitably leads judgment to pose the questions of how a maxim should be applied in particular cases; and since the answer gives us another (subordinate) maxim, we can always inquire again after a principle for applying this maxim to cases that may come up. And so ethics falls into *casuistry* . . . [which is] not so much a doctrine of how *to discover* something as rather *practice* in the proper way of *seeking* truth. Hence it is *woven into* ethics only in a *fragmentary* way, not systematically (as a part of ethics proper would have to be), and is added to ethics only as a scholia to the system.[24]

How, then, are we to bypass this endless appeal to principles, as we do in fact bypass them in real life? Having eliminated determinate theoretical understanding from the domain of ethical practice in this way,[25] judgment is left with two[26] guides. On the one hand, there is a wayward, associative picture-forming imagination which nevertheless, when tightly disciplined, may be useful for those lacking more intellectual abilities. On the other hand, there is the pure practical reason, the principles of which "contain a general determination of the will."[27] These principles do not generate any pictorial matter for the will to operate on. Indeed, if they did, they would be neither moral[28] nor rational.[29]

We should now be able to see how the problem of relativism and the theoretician's dilemma are natural consequences of drawing the distinctions between theory and practice and between reason and imagination in this way. Precisely to the extent that one's concrete choice is ethically problematic (and few today would deny that this may arise even among Kant's "perfect duties"), theoretical understanding must be abandoned. Even theoretically, universal conceptual determinations of a host of concrete ethical problems (such as those of euthanasia, abortion, and lying to hostile agents) fail to be rationally convincing.

Problems of ethical practice, on this model, are relegated to the care of practical wisdom which, in my view, is less an intelligible operation of understanding than a placeholder for a host of unresolved philosophical problems surrounding the relationship between theory and practice. To the extent that practical understanding is, in turn, understood in an Aristotelian sense as the acquisition of right habits through the repetition in practice of behavioral response patterns, moral judgment is thought to be of limited theoretical interest. But although the imagination is certainly an important feature of practical ethical judgment in this sense, I would argue that it is more than that. It is a means of ethical understanding, an essential and irreducible means by which individuals come to make the foundational (although not necessarily unalterable) distinctions which constitute the structure of their ethical interpretations.

That the self frequently finds reasons for acting for the benefit of others that are *not* derived solely from a reflection on the rationality of principle, Kant himself readily acknowledges. But he did not, I think, successfully integrate these two sorts of motivation. Having banished "inclinations" from the domain of the moral, he needs to re-establish the link between justification and motivation. At the end of *The Critique of Practical Reason*, he describes a two-step method for passing from moral judgment to moral action—i.e., "the way we can make the objectively practical reason also subjectively practical."[30]

The first step is to make judging according to moral laws a natural occupation which accompanies our own free actions as
well as our observations of those of others, and to make it, as it
were, a habit. We must sharpen these judgments by first asking
whether the action is objectively in accordance with the moral
law, and if so, with which one. . . . The second point to which
attention must be directed is the question as to whether the
action also is done (subjectively) for the sake of the moral law,
and thus not only is morally correct as a deed, but also has
moral worth as a disposition because of the maxim from which
it is done.[31]

The intention to act "for the sake of the moral law," however,
is not yet a concrete motivation. Its representation in consciousness is still that of an item of knowledge rather than a drive to
action:

But this occupation of the faculty of judgment which makes us
feel our own powers of knowledge, is not yet interest in actions
and their morality itself. It only enables one to entertain himself
with such judging and gives virtue or a turn of mind based on
moral laws a form of beauty which is admired but not yet
sought ("[Honesty] is praised and starves" [Juvenal Satire
1,74]). It is the same with everything whose contemplation produces subjectively a consciousness of the harmony of our powers of representation by which we feel our entire cognitive faculty (understanding and imagination) strengthened; it produces
a satisfaction that can be communicated to others, but the existence of its object remains indifferent to us, as it is seen only as
the occasion for our becoming aware of the store of talents
which are elevated above the mere animal level.
    Now the second exercise begins its work. It lies in calling to
notice the purity of will by a vivid exhibition of the moral disposition in examples. It is presented first only as negative perfection,
i.e., indicating that no incentives of inclinations are the determining grounds influencing an action done as duty. By this the pupils
attention is held to the consciousness of his freedom. . . .
The heart is freed from a burden which has secretly pressed
upon it; it is lightened when in instances of pure moral resolu-
tions there is revealed to man, who previously has not correctly
known it, a faculty of inner freedom to release himself from the
impetuous importunity of the inclinations, to such an extent
that not even the dearest of them has an influence on a resolution for which he now makes use of his reason. . . . The law of
duty, through the positive worth which obedience makes us feel,

finds easier access through the respect for ourselves in the consciousness of our freedom.[32]

It is just at this crucial juncture of theory and practice that Kant ends his disquisition on the methodology of pure practical reason, asserting that there only remains to be done the "prolix affair" of giving definitions of this for each moral maxim. But it is just here, I would argue, that Kant's concept of pure practical reason falls short, and where a theory of idealization is most needed. This is the moment of consciousness where moral interest originates, when we are filled with "admiration and awe" for the "moral law within me."[33]

Kant's methodology appears discontinuous at this crucial juncture. Its first step is a chapter in the natural history of consciousness, a consciousness which has become self-conscious to the extent that its questions and reflections shape its perception of situations as ethical. But the second step leaps to the pedagogical perspective and talks of pupils and examples. The rational understanding of our own conscious choices and ways of relation to others is passed over in silence.

In *The Foundations of the Metaphysics of Morals*, Kant speaks of the moment of birth of the moral interest as one of "pure respect" (or "pure reverence" in the Paton translation) for the moral law.[34] He struggles in a footnote to remove the suspicion that he has taken "refuge in an obscure feeling behind the word 'respect,' instead of clearly resolving the question with a concept of reason."[35] His answer is that respect or reverence for the moral law *is* a feeling, but one "self-wrought by a rational concept." Respect is "merely the consciousness of the submission of my will to a law without the intervention of other influences on my mind." He then adds that respect is not only the consciousness of this, but also the determination of the will by the law. He then states that respect is not only the consciousness of determination, nor merely the determination itself, but the "conception of worth" that follows from "the effect of the law on the subject"— insofar as it thwarts self-love. What seemed to be a simple concept—respect—has become overburdened with theoretical meaning. Many of these notions are provocative, but they do not yield a consistent psychology of moral feeling. Kant does not provide an adequate transition from the formal notion of law to the psychological notion of feeling. What is missing, I will argue (see

Chapter 5), is a subject-based authority in the form of a concrete ideal. Even reverence for the law is revealed to be an ideal with a history of concrete motivation and with a content which "begins at my invisible self."[36]

CHAPTER 4

The Seeing-As Concept of Imagination

Is there anything so extravagant, as the Imagination of Men's
Brains? . . . Of what use is all this fine Knowledge of Men's own
Imaginations, to a Man that enquires after the reality of Things?
John Locke, *Essay Concerning Human Understanding*[1]

INTRODUCTION

In the preceeding chapters we have described some of the confusions and ambiguities that have surrounded the concept of imagination. Yet the concept is stubborn. It resists reduction to more
familiar notions, even as it remains the focus of numerous studies
of intellectual synthesis,[2] aesthetic appreciation,[3] and creative
invention both in the sciences[4] and the arts.[5] A few studies have
attempted a systematic exposition of imagination in ethical
thought beyond the study of sympathy,[6] but the field is still relatively unexplored. The purpose of this chapter is to develop a
workable theory of the imagination suitable to the specific activity
of ethical idealization.

Given the lack of a general theory, it is far easier to describe
the structure of imaginative thought in terms of what it is not,
rather than what it is. It is not perception (the imagined object is,
at least in part, generated internally rather than produced by
external stimuli). It is not memory (it is not simply the recollec-
tion of a past psychological state). It is not belief (imagination by
itself carries no judgment of truth or falsehood). Finally, it is not
the following of a rule of reasoning, i.e., not inference (which is
not to say that it is irrational, but merely that it does not proceed
methodically).

Beyond these few negative characterizations, which are more
or less part of our commonsensical understanding of the term,
any positive development of the concept rapidly becomes contro-

versial. Meanings adapted to one domain of discourse, such as aesthetic appreciation, conflict with meanings adapted to another domain, such as scientific invention. Furthermore, even within the same domain, different theoretical interests serve to keep the notion of imagination at the level of an essentially contested concept.

The concept of imagination I will be developing is that of a *schematic* imagination, to be distinguished both from conceptualization (i.e., abstract thinking through general concepts) and mental imaging. A schematism may generate either conceptual or pictorial forms of representation, but in either case it is primarily a device of interpretation. This accords with many of our ways of using the term, but certainly not all. Other uses of the word are common. We frequently talk of imagining when we mean pretending, supposing, surmising, hypothesizing, theorizing, postulating, guessing, assuming, entertaining, conjecturing, or speculating. Most of these are assimilated by the categories of description, explanation, and narrative. Although a full theory of imagination would need to provide an account of them, they can at this time be left in the background. To distinguish these and other uses from the notion of schematic imagination, I will refer to them (following Casey and Ryle) as either "imagining-that," or "imagining-how."[7]

Controversy also surrounds the link between imagination and creativity (itself a highly contested concept). To many, the two terms are virtually identical. I would like, however, to keep them distinct. For the purpose of adapting a concept of imagination to that of ethical idealization, the creativity of our ideals is a secondary and perhaps even irrelevant consideration—at least if we take creativity in its common meaning as innovation or the production of novelty. Indeed, innovation (i.e., the production of new routines) has, I believe, been over-emphasized as a feature of imagination. There is no *prima facie* reason why imagination in itself should be regarded as more innovative than inference. Descartes'[8] adherence to logical inference in the *Meditations*, for example, was far more productive of new routines of thought than the random generation of new images by an aspiring avant-garde painter would be. Other senses of the word *creativity*, however, may be more closely aligned with the imagination—creativity in the sense of 'originality,' not in the sense of 'productive of the different,' but in the sense of 'linked to origins.'

WITTGENSTEIN'S CONCEPT OF SEEING-AS

The concept of imagination I wish to develop takes its point of departure from the notion of "seeing-as." The *locus classicus* for this concept is Wittgenstein's *Philosophical Investigations*, II, xi.[9] The concept points to a process, momentary or sustained, and to a greater or lesser degree within one's conscious control, of altering one's perceptions and perspectives so as to have varying experiences of a single object. Wittgenstein talks of it as (newly) noticing an aspect (p. 193). Necker cubes and Jastrow's duck-rabbits are the laboratory paradigms, but examples may also be readily drawn from ordinary experience (e.g., seeing a face in a crowd as the face of one's friend). Beginning with the simple idea that noticing an aspect is a matter of seeing a likeness, Wittgenstein develops the notion that seeing-as is a special work of the imagination. Being struck by an aspect, particularly an "aspect of organization," is inexplicable in traditional epistemological categories: "Is being struck looking plus thinking? No. Many of our concepts *cross* here" (p. 211).

Wittgenstein's discussion is provocative and exploratory rather than constructive and systematic. He is on the trail of an idea which reveals its place among the concepts of experience, not because it possesses a clear theoretical meaning but because we apparently have certain experiences which cannot be explained in other terms. The examples of seeing-as that Wittgenstein uses are varied: duck-rabbit figures, a doll treated as human by a child, seeing the lines in a puzzle-picture as a human shape, seeing an old man as one's childhood friend, seeing a triangle as a mountain or wedge or arrow or pointer, seeing a picture as a sphere floating in the air, seeing the vowel *a* as a blue sound, hearing a musical bar as an introduction, seeing a portrait as though it were smiling at you, hearing a musical theme as not quite a dance, seeing someone's posture as hesitant, hearing a melody as plaintive, seeing a child as like his father, seeing a photograph as a representation *of* something, reading a set of lines as a poem, hearing the word *bank* as riverbank rather than financial bank, thinking of the idea of Wednesday as fat and the idea of Tuesday as lean, sensing "a word on the tip of one's tongue" as just the right word for something.

It is doubtful that all these cases are amenable to the same precise analysis, but they serve to draw attention to a peculiar experience halfway between perception and conceptual thought.

Wittgenstein calls it an "amalgam" of the two. Some of the examples are closer to perception, and others are closer to thought and inference, but none are purely either.

A feature that distinguishes at least most of these cases from perception is the presence of a certain element of control that seems to be lacking in ordinary perception:

> Seeing an aspect and imagining are subject to the will. There is such an order as "Imagine *this*," and also: "Now see the figure like *this*"; but not: Now see this leaf green." (p. 213)

> "Now I see it as a . . . " goes with "I am trying to see it as a . . . or "I can't see it as a . . . yet." But I cannot see a conventional picture of a lion *as* a lion, any more than an *F* as that letter. (Though I may well try to see it as a gallows, for example . . .) (p. 206)

On the other hand, the control is not the kind that we have over what we *think* as distinguished from what we perceive. Seeing-as remains pre-inferential:

> A *concept* forces itself on one. (This is what you must not forget.) . . . "To me it is an animal pierced by an arrow." That is what I treat it as; this is my *attitude* to the figure. This is one meaning in calling it a case of "seeing."

This is particularly significant for those cases of seeing-as which lean toward what has traditionally been called fantasy or make-believe. A child playing a game, for example, may see a chest of drawers as a house:

> "He quite forgets that it is a chest; for him it is actually a house." (There are definite tokens of this.) Then would it not also be correct to say that he *sees* it as a house? (p. 206)

The child is doing something more than simply redescribing (although he is certainly doing that also). Depending on the seriousness of his game, he sees the chest *as* a house: it *is* a house in his game.

The idea of a controlled perception is an elusive one, for our traditional categories of experience lead us to treat control as something we exercise *after* perception is 'given.' In the absence of a theory of imagination, there is a tendencey to force cases of seeing-as into the categories of either mistaken belief or of make-believe and fantasy. In turn, both of these latter categories are aligned with the notion of perceptual error—with the result that what is imagined in this way is contrasted with what is true. And given our habit of treating perception as passive, the analysis of mistaken belief leads naturally into the Cartesian consclusion that error is a misuse of judgment. Judgment for Descartes is a combination of understanding plus will. And because both of these are perfect faculties given by God, they could not in themselves be responsible for error.

> Whence, then, arise my errors? From this fact alone, that the will being much more ample and extended than the understanding, I do not contain it within the same limits, but extend it also to things that I do not understand, and the will being of itself indifferent to such things, very easily goes astray and chooses the bad instead of the good, or the false instead of the true, which results in my falling into error or sinning.[10]

In the Cartesian framework, those cases of seeing-as which are typically analyzed as cases of mistaken belief are accounted for in terms of a misuse of the will. If one only kept one's inferences within the bounds prescribed by method, truth would be assured. But the examples adduced by Wittgenstein make this an implausible absolute. The categories of will and belief are too blunt-edged to rationalize the fine-grained processing of experience involved here. Furthermore, mistaken perceptions seem to entail a belief, whereas as seeing-as does not. If one takes a tree at night to *be* a burgler, one is psychologically committed to the belief that it *is* a burgler. But one can see it *as* a burgler without a corresponding belief commitment. The element of control at the level of perception distinguishes seeing-as from mistaken perceptions and gives it the genuine character of imagination. It would be a mistake to say, for example, that the child playing the game has a mistaken belief about what is real, as it would be a mistake for two people to argue over whether the Jastrow figure were *really* a duck or a rabbit. Seeing-as is not simply a matter of the will exceeding the understanding.

Equally, seeing-as is not simply a matter of what an early empiricist such as Locke would call idle fancy, irrelevant to the truth of things. One's ultimate view on this depends, of course, on what one means by truth and reality. But a theory of imagination need not be bound up with such large metaphysical issues. No claim is being made concerning the metaphysical status of imagined objects. Whether they are real or not will be decided on grounds other than the mere fact that they are imagined. Ethical seeing-as (e.g., seeing a person as worthy of respect) is prior to, and comparable with, a range of philosophical ontologies of the person.

Nothing seems to be gained, either, by a Romantic typology which urges a sharp distinction between fantasy *qua* delusion and imagination proper, which is meant to provide access to transcendental realities. The insistence by Romantic writers that the objects of a legitimate imagination (i.e., one which maintains its connections with the concept of truth) are radically discontinuous with the objects of ordinary experience has done much to dilute the value of the concept as an important category among the concepts of experience. The bracketing of ordinary experience in a game may be of a different level than the bracketing which occurs at high levels of creative inspiration, but it is not of an essentially different type. The exoticism behind such transcendental interpretations of imagination seems to stem from the assumption that what we imagine (properly) commits us to a belief in its literal truth: if it lacks an object in ordinary experience, it must therefore have one in a transcendental realm.

Ironically, very *un*romantic writers such as Freud and Sartre, who have been concerned to show how much our so-called ordinary experience is filled with unreal products of the imagination, have also contributed to the erosion of the value of the concept except as a term for unconscious pathology. Sartre writes:

> We have seen that the act of the imagination is a magical one. It is an incantation destined to produce the object of one's thought, the thing one desires, in a manner that one can take possession of it. In that act there is always something of the imperious and the infantile, a refusal to take distance or difficulties into account. . . . For the rest, the object of an image is an unreality. It is no doubt present, but, at the same time, it is out of reach. I cannot touch it, change its place: or rather I can well do so, but on condition that I do it in an unreal way, by not using my own hands but those of some phantomns which give this face unreal blows: to act upon these unreal objects I must divide myself, make myself *unreal*.[11]

Sartre's identification of the imaginary and the unreal is, as Ishiguro[12] has pointed out, a somewhat perverse reading of the psychological facts. The key distinction for a theory of imagination is not between the real and the unreal, but between the literal and the metaphorical. Imagination requires neither the presence nor absence of a perceived object. Nothing essential about the nature of imaginative operations is determined by whether their data are supplied by direct perception or by memory or some other source. In each case it is the seeing-as operation which is crucial.

A more minimal conception of truth is sufficient to extricate a viable concept of imaginative perception from the epistemologically disreputable notion of fantasy. Internal to one's interpretive world, a distinction can rationally be drawn between imaginative seeings-as which are congruent with the objects of one's developing understanding and those which are not. It is in this sense that we may speak of some imaginative endeavors as having a truth to them and others as lacking this truth.

In characterizing the imagination as seeing-as, I am making the claim that it is a form of understanding. The notion of seeing is wider than that of visualizing (e.g., "I see your point"). To see—in the wide sense I wish to use—is to make distinctions in an object. In saying this, I am urging that we resist the persuasive rhetoric of Ryle:

> There is no special Faculty of Imagination, occupying itself single-mindedly in fancied viewings and hearings. On the contrary, "seeing" things is one exercise of imagination, growling somewhat like a bear is another; smelling things in the mind's nose is an uncommon act of fancy, malingering is a very common one, and so forth. . . . Indeed, if we are asked whether imagining is a cognitive or non-cognitive activity, our proper policy is to ignore the question. "Cognitive" belongs to the vocabulary of examination papers.[13]

But to treat imagination as a human capacity—something that humans, as contrasted with nonconscious beings, are able to do—is not the same as embracing a medieval faculty theory. Furthermore, the contrast between seeing and doing is rhetorical (playing on an ambiguity between doing and bodily movement). Imagination is a doing which is a seeing. Growling like a bear is not an exercise of the imagination if one is a bear or if one's stomach is rumbling. To imagine is to make certain kinds of interpretive distinctions in one's world, and this is indeed a cognitive activity—even if we are not yet able to say how such an activity best fits into a theory of knowledge and rationality.

Now even this conception of imagination requires a developed theory which recognizes that what we regard as the primary characteristics of an object will differ with our interpretive and historical starting points. Wittgenstein's discussion offers little in the way of constructive theory on this point. He does, however, indicate that seeing-as is to be distinguished from fantasy and make-believe, if these are understood as forms of arbitrary invention. In most of his examples, seeing X as Y is constrained in part by objective features of X. One can fail to distinguish those features and so suffer from aspect-blindness: "Aspect blindness will be *akin* to the lack of a 'musical ear.'"[14]

SCHEMATISMS OF INTERPRETATION

Further development of the concept of a schematism leads us to other disciplines. A full account would need to show the psychological roots behind varying kinds of schematic discrimination as well as give some account of the cognitive processes involved. The latter is the focus of considerable attention in the work of cognitive psychologists, work such as Allan Paivio's dual coding approach.[15] Pertinent also (although also outside the scope of this work) would be the elaboration of the semantics of metaphor involved (the "as" side of seeing-as).[16]

The schematism structures meaning by mediating between the concrete level of perception (understood in the wide sense to include not merely sensory perception, but situational perception—e.g., "I see that you are upset") and the abstract level of conception. I use the term *conception* in a psychological sense rather than a logical sense. Schemas generate models of a set of related concepts. A concept is a mental representation (or model) of a category, which functions to sort stimuli into psychological objects. A concept is the psychological meaning of a word. A category is a semantic specification of a concept, which functions to generate a class of logical objects.[17] A concept is no wider than the set of instances which are understood to fall under it. If I have not imagined airplanes, then my concept of *vehicle* as *traveling device* does not include airplanes, even though an airplane logically falls under the category of vehicles. As a psychological object, a concept may include much information extraneous to (and even logically incon-sistent with) its corresponding category—e.g., "pleasant to go to the beach in" or "limited to a speed of 100 miles an hour."

Concepts differ from categories in other important ways. Unlike categories, concepts (and, for that matter, images) are structured by salience cues: certain examples of a concept are treated by the mind as more paradigmatic, more significant than other examples which are of the same logical level. A collection of these more salient properties is called a *prototype*. An implication of this is that, if the schematism structures meaning by discover-ing a fit between perception and conception, and conception is prototypically organized, then moral learning may occur more profoundly through the incorporation into the self of exemplars and examples that fit that prototype than through the learning and application of moral rules.[18]

This mediating role of the schematism was pointed out by Kant in his theory of imagination. But Kant placed three limita-tions on the role of imagination, all of which I wish to remove. First, in his theory of *reproductive* imagination, he saw the role of the schematism as supplying concepts for images gained solely from sensory perception. I believe the term can be usefully extended to cover cases of pre-interpreted perceptions, such as perceiving that a situation is dangerous, or that an institution is overextended, or that an action is wrong. Second, Kant limited the synthetic unity of apperception achieved by the *productive* imagination to an intuition of selfhood as a purely regulative transcendental idea. It is a thesis of this book, however, that the self is genuinely knowable in experience—not, of course, merely as a representation (since it is also structural), but in the experi-ence of growth, restoration, and integration that accompanies a life in which ideals are harmonized with ambitions. Third, Kant limited the *creative* imagination to aesthetic productions, under-stood as the appreciation of the beautiful and sublime dimensions of experience. I wish to treat the creative power of imagination as a much broader facility; the term is equally appropriate in the case of the ethical productions of human beings, namely, their ideals. Kant's romantic category of *genius* as the "faculty of aes-thetical ideas"[19] forces an unnecessary rift between moral and aesthetic experience.[20] The ordinary moral life of ordinary human beings uses the same capacity of imagination as does the produc-tion and appreciation of art.

Both the psychology and the semantics of seeing-as are use-fully developed through the notion of a schematism of interpreta-tion. Let us return to an example of Wittgenstein's—seeing a tri-angle as a mountain, or a wedge, or a pointer. How are we to describe the process of searching for and discovering the new rep-resentation? To the degree that it is within our control, the opera-tion is a conscious one. Part of the answer can no doubt be given in terms of a matching process: similarities are discovered between these objects and the triangle on the page. Indeed, for Aristotle, similarity is the heart of metaphor. At the end of the *Poetics*, after discussing the specific poetic techniques of Aeschy-lus and Euripides, he concludes:

> It is a great thing, indeed, to make a proper use of these poetical forms, as also of compounds and strange words. But the great-est thing by far is to be a master of metaphor. It is the one thing that cannot be learnt from others; and it is also a sign of genius, since a good metaphor implies an intuitive perception of the similarity in dissimilars.[21]

But more is involved, since the second term of the similarity rela-tion is lacking a determinate representation in consciousness. When Wittgenstein says that to see X as Y is an exercise of the imagination,[22] he cannot simply be taken to mean that one notices a similarity. More is involved in seeing a triangle as a mountain, wedge, or pointer than this. The mind plays a more productive role. Wittgenstein's analysis is helpfully developed by Wilkerson, who introduces the notion of a constructed back-ground:

> It is rather as if, in *seeing* it *as* one or more of those things, one is *providing* a further point of similarity, by using one's imagina-tion. To put the point rather crudely, it is as if one is mentally constructing a certain background, into which the triangle might fit—perhaps imagining it to be suspended from a hook in the middle of a physical laboratory, or to be covered with snow in the middle of an Alpine massif, or to be embedded in a crack in a piece of wood, ready to be hit with a hammer. It is almost as if one were drawing in a hook, or a range of mountains, or a hammer and piece of wood.[23]

Seeing an aspect, then, may be said to involve the construction of a background against which the feature in question attains salience. We may think of these constructed backgrounds as imaginative schemas—large units of cognition within which objects are apprehended according to certain aspects. Such schemas operate not merely at the sensory level (the visual and auditory, for example), but are equally operative in such domains as the theoretical, the ethical, the aesthetic, and the prudential. And where the imagination is attentive to objectivities rather than being merely arbitrary, something in the constructed background has a truth to it, the mind sees the invented context as appropriate in some way to what it takes to be the real nature of the thing perceived.

Speaking of pictorial art, E. H. Gombrich[24] speaks of such a background as a "matrix" within which the structural relationships of a picture are perceived. We see Mondrian's *Broadway Boogie-Woogie* as a picture of wild exuberance when placed in the matrix of Mondrian's restrained style as he made his aesthetic choices in communication with his culture. But if we were to see the same picture as if it were painted by Severini, famous for his luxuriant and rythmic forms, we might think *Bach's First Brandenburg Concerto* a more apt title for the piece.

Gombrich's point can be extended beyond the relation between images and what they represent. What is at issue is our ways of seeing and interpreting. Echoing Wittgenstein's remark that our categories of looking and thinking "cross" at certain points, Gombrich concludes that

> we can never neatly separate what we see from what we know. A person who was born blind, and who gains eyesight later on, must *learn* to see. With some self-discipline and self-observation we can all find out for ourselves that what we call seeing is invariably coloured and shaped by our knowledge (or belief) of what we see. . . . In fact, as soon as we start to take a pencil and draw, the whole idea of surrendering passively to what is called our sense impressions becomes really an absurdity. If we look out of the window we can see the view in a thousand different ways. Which of them is our sense impression?[25]

Schematisms have a picturing mode of operation, just as they have an explanatory or descriptive mode, but to say this is not the same as advocating a theory of mental images. Imagination may often involve the production of mental images, although this is certainly not a requirement. As Ishiguro notes:

> Mental images are, at most, necessary tools for a *limited number* of people in *certain kinds* of exercise of the imagination and

are, for many people, merely psychological accompaniments which occur when they are engaged in imaginative work and not the essence of it.[26]

Not all pictorial theories accept the notion of mental imagery. Sartre, for example, responding to certain metaphysical excesses and theoretical limitations of some mental-image theories, treats imagination as a modality of consciousness rather than the generation of an image object.[27] Ishiguro agrees;[28] "The fact that I picture something does not entail that I see a mental picture of the thing."

Certainly the notion of pictorial production through schema is *wider* than that of mental imagery.[29] The complexity of its operation 'behind the scenes' of the representational structure led Kant to call it "an art concealed in the depths of the human soul, whose real modes of activity nature is hardly likely ever to allow us to discover, and to have open to our gaze."[30] Such an intuition has no doubt been the motivation not only of those theories of imagination which reject mental images altogether, but also of the traditional typological distinctions of the past three centuries (imagination vs. fantasy, primary vs. secondary imagination, productive vs. reproductive imagination, and so on). On this point, contemporary theory is in a formative stage and a general specification would be premature. The task is best approached piecemeal, according to the context in which the imagination functions. The present project is restricted to imagination's role in ethical idealization. It should be clear, however, that acknowledging a place for mental images in imagination does not entail the adoption of any form of representative theory of perception, in which images are in some way mimetic copies of real things. Several theories of pictorial representation other than the mimetic are presently available.[31]

Wittgenstein himself does tie the concept of seeing-as to entities in the mind which he calls images:

> The concept of an aspect is akin to the concept of an image. In other words" the concept "I am now seeing it as . . . " is akin to "I am now having *this* image."[32]

Why he makes this connection is unclear. It seems an unnecessary limitation on an otherwise extremely valuable concept. It invokes all the epistemological problems of the 'idea' idea, while offering little in return. Part of the reason may have been a lingering attachment to an empiricist dogma of passive perception. In analyzing an ambiguous figure, Wittgenstein asks:

> Do I really see something different each time, or do I only interpret what I see in a different way? I am inclined to say the former. But why?—To interpret is to think, to do something; seeing is a state. (p. 212)

The implication is that seeing is passive. In treating perception as passive, Wittgenstein is led to regard the active side of seeing-as as purely conceptual. He therefore narrows the concept of interpretation to that of inference and hypothesis formation. But this excludes the synthesizing function of interpretation which, I believe, has as one of its possibilities a genuine picture-generating function.

Wittgenstein's doctrine that meaning is use penetrates deeply into his analysis of seeing-as. It leads him to maintain a sharp difference between seeing and interpreting at the level of meaning, while "amalginating" it at the level of experience:

> Now it is easy to recognize cases in which we are *interpreting*. When we interpret we form hypotheses, which may prove false.—"I am seeing this figure as a . . . " can be verified as little as (or in the same sense as) "I am seeing bright red." So there is a similarity in the use of "seeing" in the two contexts. Only do not think you knew in advance what the "*state* of seeing" means here! Let the use *teach* you the meaning. (p. 212)

In consequence, Wittgenstein is led to the view that the semantic content of seeing-as is not to be clarified by the analysis of conscious experience. When, for example, I tell someone to "Wait for me by the bank," I may picture to myself a particular bank on a particular street. We might be tempted, on later reflection, to say that this picturing was part of our conscious experience, part of what we *meant* or *intended*. But this, for Wittgenstein, is the mistake of reading into the experience our later interpretation:

> Meaning is as little an experience as intending. But what distinguishes them from experience?—They have no experience-content. For the contents (images for instance) which accompany and illustrate them are not the meaning or intending. (p. 217)

Again:

> "The impression was that of a rearing animal." So a perfectly
> definite description came out.—Was it a *seing* or was it a
> thought? Do not try to analyse your own inner experience. (p.
> 204)

And again:

> "The word is on the tip of my tongue." What is going on in my
> consciousness? That is not the point at all. Whatever did go on
> was not what was meant by that expression. It is of more inter-
> est what went on in my behaviour.—The word is on the tip of
> my tongue" tells you: the word which belongs here has escaped
> me, but I hope to find it soon. . . . But this is not experience at
> all. *Interpreted* as experience it does indeed look odd (p. 219).

Wittgenstein's methodological and metaphysical presuppositions prohibit him from looking for an explication of this through
an analysis of consciousness. For Wittgenstein, consciousness is
experiential (i.e., its data are what is seen *through* ones' structure
of interpretation, not operations *on* that structure). He is driven
by his caveat that meaning derives from use to look for an explication in behavior and situational context.

On a wider acceptation of rational interpretation, however,
the exclusion of the analysis of conscious experience seems arbitrary, the relic of a positivism that has been elsewhere abandoned.
Human rationality simple is not restricted to hypothetico-deduc-
tive operations on experimental or clinical data. A concrete reflection is at work in the midst of experience and action which draws
on the synthesizing and schematizing operations which define our
concept of the imagination. The truth of the matter is that our
concepts and models may mean more or less than we are aware,
and language-games may be well-formed or ill-structured. Both
great discoveries and tragic dead ends may lurk at the borders of
our various language games. These could not be discovered, could
not even be named, were inner experience to be excluded as a
source of meaning. We arrive at these territories precisely through
an experience in which the data of experience and the self's inner
meanings are intimately caught up, in which the meaning of the
one informs and illuminates the other.

A schematizing imagination bridges the absolute gap between
the abstract and the concrete which has become so much a part of

our thinking about thinking. At all levels of thought (not just the perceptual level), schematic imagination *forms* the objects of our world, rather than abstracts *from* them. Schemas[33] generate our modeling of the world, with greater or less specificity. They are mental 'sets,' more or less alterable, to interpret a given range of objects one way or another (e.g., the famous duck-rabbit and Necker cube schemas). Schemas have a different 'logic' than the logic of concepts. Being contextually grounded, they lack a rule of universalization. From the fact that I see a set of lines in one context as a rabbit, nothing follows regarding how I will see the same set of lines in a different context.

The cognitive space of these schemas lacks an a priori determination, not only because the objects are perceived and interpreted according to certain cultural styles of object formation, but also because the space itself receives a significant part of its structure from the very objects which are 'contained' in it. It is not as if one person comes to the Jastrow figure with a pre-existing determinate duck schema and another person comes with a similar rabbit schema. An infinite variety of psychological sets are compatible with seeing the figure as a duck or a rabbit. If no Jastrow figure were encountered, we could not meaningfully say that such a person has a duck or a rabbit schema. The space receives part of its structure from the encounter itself. Such a space may certainly be structured by concepts but, to borrow a phrase of Ricoeur's, they are concepts used "in a pictorial mode": the objects delineated within that space are the concrete objects of psychological apprehension rather than the abstract objects of a universal logic.

Considered from the point of view of its objects, imagination may be thought of as the act of bringing particular features of experience to the attention of consciousness. In this respect, seeing-as is that dimension of the schematizing imagination which emerges as the concrete activity of noticing an aspect. It addresses a particular object or situation, not indirectly as an instance of a law, but directly and immediately as possessed of a certain characteristic. Considered from the point of view of its pre-representational operation, however, seeing-as is the act of schematization, of arranging the structure of the mental space in which the objects of experience appear. This notion of mental space is, of course, metaphorical—and densely so: it carries with it not only the connotations of contour and form, but also what Ricoeur has termed a "quasi-corporeal exteriority."[34] But mental space is not a domain that we inhabit like a mollusc in the sea; it *is* us. If a theory of schematic representation is to be made intelligible, the notion of space must be given a philosophical and psychological exposition rather than left at the level of a figure.

CHAPTER 5

Ethical Ideals

> [T]here is nothing absolutely ideal: ideals are relative to the lives
> that entertain them. To keep out of the gutter is for us here no part
> of consciousness at all, yet for many of our bretheren it is the most
> legitimately engrossing of ideals.
>
> William James, *Talks to Teachers*[1]

THE NATURE OF IDEALS

The theory of a schematizing imagination developed in the pre-
ceding chapter provides a framework for a theory of ideals. Ideals
are imaginative envisionings of the good life or, more precisely,
procedures for interpreting the world and organizing one's
responses to it in terms of what the self takes to be its good life.
They may function at varying levels of reflection, from the grand
level of utopian theory to the *minutiae* of our daily lives.
Although we require a certain height and dignity of our ideals,
they frequently function without the demand for absolute perfection.[2] They generate models of the kinds of persons we would like
to be, the kinds of relations we would like to have with others,
and the kind of world we would like to live in. Ideals may vary
from person to person, and from culture to culture. And they may
stem from a variety of motivations ranging from the pathological
to the saintly.

Psychologically, ideals possess a dual aspect, operating as
both a structure of interpretation and a structure of motivation.
They are interpretive processes which link the description of
objects to our scheme of values so as to produce a response. As
structures of interpretation, they perform the schematic seeing-as
function, enabling one to interpret *A* as *B*. This function precedes
both imaging and conceptualization. Ideals frequently generate
images and ideas of the good life, but it is the psychological structures which generate these images and ideas—not the representa-

tions themselves—which are the ideals. Images or descriptions of admired states and persons are, from the point of view of their depth-psychology, secondary. Such representations play a role, of course, in idealization, but they are psychologically inert. The exhortation to 'be like that!' accompanies only genuine ideals produced by imagination in its schematic function.

So considered, an ideal is *not* a fantasized vision of perfection which one uses to evaluate a flawed reality, but a way of perceiving existing reality. In idealization we see a situation not simply descriptively, but as more or less ideal. Ideality and actuality are not to be seen as metaphysically distinct, the former describing what one *would like*, while the latter describes *what is*. Rather, idealization is one of the ways that one perceives *what is*. An important consequence of this is that traditional distinctions between prescription and description, between *is* and *ought*, between will and inclination, begin to break down.

Ideals are not principles. Principles are general imperatives of right behavior. 'Do not kill' expresses a principle; 'the end of war on our planet' expresses an ideal. 'Provide for your family' expresses a principle; 'a house in the suburbs for my family' expresses an ideal. Principles and ideals have different logics. Principles are conceptual and universalizable. Ideals are schematic and tied to the aims of the concrete self. Although they may be shared, ideals are not universalizable. From the fact that one person holds an ideal, it does not follow that he thereby prescribes that all persons hold that ideal.

Ideals occupy a semantic space halfway between general principles and particular descriptions. They are neither purely deducible from the *ought* of principle, nor inductively derivable from the *is* of circumstance. In idealization there is a free play of concepts and imagery, which makes a theory of imagination an appropriate method for its analysis. In the process of idealization, our inherited and unreflective understandings of the right and the true are in an important sense suspended. Aesthetic and speculative possibilities are permitted to mold our ideals in a way we do not permit either our understanding of principle or our apprehension of fact. On the other hand, this play has a seriousness to it which distinguishes it from fantasy and daydreaming. The self is intimately involved in the capacity of both observer and agent of this play, and is *at stake*. Identity is at issue—not the partial and ultimately illusory identity of defensive ego structures, but true self-identity, the dynamic identity of self-representation with self-structure as it seeks its good life. For this reason, ideals (although they are free creations) carry *authority* for the self: they prescribe precisely because they describe the ends of one's own-most self.

Ideals are both a way of ordering our objective experience and a form of reflected self-understanding which can translate, within the structure of the self, into motivation. Seeing-as, the schematism, is the 'outer' dimension and refers to the self's interpretation of its environment. There is also the 'inner' dimension, which involves alterations within the structure of the self in terms of identification, incorporation, introjection, and internalization. That these two aspects are intimately linked is attested to by a great deal of psychoanalytic and psychological literature, beginning with Freud's early concept of the ego as built on the residue of past identifications. An enormous amount of clinical observation has revealed that our experience of objects (particularly person-objects—those perceived parts of persons which we selectively incorporate into ourselves) and structure-building processes within the self are closely connected and cannot ultimately be treated separately.

Not all ideals are ethical ideals, of course, although it is not at all easy to say what it is about some ideals that marks them as ethical. For one thing, the question is only partly an objective question (whereas the question of whether certain actions fall under certain principles is entirely an objective question). There are two reasons for this. First, as already noted, the nature and significance of ideals varies between cultures and persons. Second, even granting that the objects of ideals differ, there is more to ethical ideals than their objects. Equally important is the way that the ideal is incorporated into one's character, how it functions as a counter in ratiocination, and how it operates in the subjective experience and motivation of the individual. Envisioning a city without homeless people may simply be daydreaming rather than ethical idealization. Even acting on that vision does not distinguish it as ethical (e.g., if one does so to advance one's political career). And even acting 'for the sake of the ideal itself' is not an analytically primitive notion, not a place at which ethical theory can rest. (One's commitment to something's 'sake' could, after all, be subject to distortions ranging from conceptual misconstruals to the pathologies of fanaticism.) The structure of the reflection which creates and sustains the ideal, in both its subjective and objective aspects, must be investigated.

If this is correct, the investigation of this serious play of the ethical imagination must take us beyond the *logic* of morals—beyond the analysis of the conceptual structure of our moral representations—to the *psychology* of morals (the study of the relations between moral representations and the concrete structure of the person).[3] For what gives ideals their peculiarly ethical character is not merely their content but also the way in which that content is held. A constructive theory of ethical ideals, therefore, needs to attend to the realities of psychological motivation: to their origin in the nuclear structures of the developing self; to their shaping by socio-psychological factors; and to the processes of reflective self-understanding through which ideals are owned and authentically incorporated by the mature and conscious self.

KIERKEGAARD'S APPROACH TO ETHICAL IDEALIZATION

Kierkegaard is one of the few philosophers to probe the concrete structure of self-reflection that occurs in ethical idealization. In *Either/Or* he displays the contradictory alternatives of the aesthetic and ethical lives. Each life is built upon a relationship between the actual self and an imagined possibility. In volume two, Judge William, representing the ethical life, pinpoints the different starting points of these imaginative acts. The aesthete begins his reflection from a point of view external to his actual self. He "views himself in his concretion and then distinguishes *inter et inter*. He regards some things as belonging to him accidentally, other things as belonging to him essentially."[4]

He then chooses the essential as his life-possibility. But he is betrayed by his starting points, his already defined identity, and finds no true vocation to action. The choice is illusory since the 'essential' elements that he chooses have begun their life outside of the concretely reflecting consciousness and reveal themselves as representations only "for so long as a man lives merely aesthetically one thing belongs to him as accidentally as another, and it is merely for lack of energy an aesthetic individual maintains this distinction."[5]

The aesthetically structured personality constantly suffers the temptation to passively flee into fanciful possibility in an attempt to negate the finite limitations of his actual 'accidental' life.[6]

In ethical imagination, on the other hand, the ideal self emerges from the reflective representations of the actual self:

> He who lives ethically abolishes to a certain degree the distinction between the accidental and the essential, for he accepts himself, every inch of him, as equally essential. But the distinction returns, for when he has done this he distinguishes again, yet in such a way that for the accidental which he excludes he accepts an essential responsibility for excluding it.[7]

In this way, says Kierkegaard, the ideal self is "infinitized" in the imagination as passion, thereby maintaining the inner connection between the actual and ideal self. This is an existential passion, not an emotion, and it does not require regular episodes of sympathetic sentiment. Pseudonymously (as Johannes Climacus), he expounds elsewhere:

> It is only momentarily that the particular individual is able to realize existentially a unity of the infinite and the finite which transcends existence. . . . In passion the existing subject is rendered infinite in the eternity of the imaginative representation, and yet he is at the same time most definitely himself.[8]

For Kierkegaard, the ethical significance of idealization lies solely in the moment of choice. It has nothing to do with the particular content of the ideal.

> But what is it I choose? Is it this thing or that? No, for I choose absolutely, and the absoluteness of my choice is expressed precisely by the fact that I have not chosen to choose this or that. I choose the absolute. And what is the absolute? It is I myself in my eternal validity. Anything else but myself I never can choose as the absolute, for if I choose something else, I choose it as a finite thing and so do not choose it absolutely.[9]

Seen from the side of its origination, the ethicality of the ideal is a consequence of the individual's choice of his full actuality as his essential reality: not in the sense of putting up with the conditions he finds himself in, but in the sense of acknowledging that his own actuality is the source of the significance of those conditions through an ideality lying within himself:

> What then is the real? It is the ideality. But aesthetically and intellectually the ideality is the possible (the translation from *esse ad posse*). Ethically the ideality is the real within the individual himself. The real is an inwardness that is infinitely interested in existing; this is exemplified in the ethical individual.[10]

But the infinitizing process of idealization has a teleological dimension as well; otherwise its freedom would remain abstract. Kierkegaard thus postulates a second movement in which the ideal self is involved in "an infinite coming back to itself in the finitizing process."[11] Cumming writes:

> Where the aesthetic stage exhibits in retrospect the inconclusive-ness of the process of reflection and the indefiniteness of a mere point of view, the ethical stage exhibits the process of reaching a "definite position" as a conclusion, by making a choice which is decisive.[12]

In this way, for Kierkegaard, a determination may be reached—not by choosing 'the nature of things' as in Stoicism, but (as it were) by choosing to choose oneself in an imaginatively lived life. David Gouwens reveals how permeated by the imagination are each of these movements of the ethical consciousness:

> Not only is the imagination now the servant of the concrete as well as the possible, but the imagination, which in art distances and so yields only an "external infinity," now in the ethical life ironically opens up the realm of the "inner infinite" for which art yearns. In ethical subjectivity, the imagination provides the abstraction from the given, and so "internally' generates an "external" ethical ideal which as a goal that is acted upon becomes truly "internal." The ideal is my ideal, and yet it stands apart from me as my goal; it is an external goal, and yet it points to the concrete self I strive to become. Ethical subjectiv-ity, in short, fulfills the dreams of art.[13]

Kierkegaard (through his pseudonyms) offers a number of rich insights into the structure of ethical reflection, particularly regard-ing its starting points. He demonstrates that, if the ideal is to retain its links to motivation, rather than merely being an 'abstract possi-bility,' the understanding of it must include an awareness (in a manner yet to be made clear) that the ideal is in some sense *who one actually is*. The ethicality of an ideal is to be sought in the con-crete structure of the person. Yet the sparse dialectics of the exis-tentialist doctrine of choice present grave problems for a viable account of inner ethical life. The ethical individual, for Kierkegaard, is supremely isolated at both crucial ethical moments: at the moment when he imagines his ideal self, and at the juncture of reflection and action. Kierkegaard robustly embraces this isola-tion as definitional of ethicality itself. Yet this fails, I think, to account for two key features of the ethical situation. First, it leaves suspended the individual's relation to the moral tradition (its principles, practices, and procedures) both in terms of rationality relations and authority relations. This generates an enormous problem of justification.[14] Secondly, it severs the psychological links necessary for community with others, both affectively in terms of sympathy and effectively in terms of cooperative action. Ethics must finally have to do with our relation to others as persons. If the motivation for other-directed action is to remain viable, the imaginative transformations in the concrete structure of the self that psychologically define ethical idealization must be essentially mediated by representations of that community.

A genuine ethical ideal must sustain the connection between justification and motivation. Kierkegaard rightly insists that this requires us to leave the abstract level of principle to probe the concrete structure of the person. But the dialectics of absolute disjunction in his 'either/or' are insufficient foundation for an adequate concept of ethical imagining.

The choice faced by a rational being concerned to be moral is not between idealization and reality (whether reality is understood as advancement of self-interest, obedience to the moral law, or calm estimation of welfare consequences). The choice is this: given that what we know as reality is shaped by ideals, *which* ideals are we going to pursue, and in what manner? Kierkegaard was one of the few who tried to provide an account of this ideational dimension of the ethical project. But he tried to do it solely in terms of the dialectics of subjective choice. He was led to this because he had no theory of the structure of the self which went beyond the bare disjunctive moment of ethical choice, either/or. The self was for Kierkegaard (as it is for existentialism in general) a vanishing point. Kierkegaard gives a masterly representation of the play of self-schema in the situation of ethical choice, and much of it remains psychologically valid. But he does not, and could not, pursue that play beyond the self's subjectivity to its developing relation with others. The limitation of Kierkegaard's approach is that, although it maintains the component of desire in ethics, it does so only by abandoning rationality at key points. Kierkegaard, while recognizing that our ideals are not compulsive and are to be located in the domain of the self's freedom, nevertheless lacked an adequate psychology of the self. This produced an unnecessarily mysterious model of the space of moral freedom where the inner dynamics between concrete and ideal self could only be explained in terms of a vertiginous either/or in which rationality could gain no foothold. The truth is, however, that freedom is not a vacuum; it teems with structure. The attempt by existentialists to ignore this is revealed as a mistake by their ongoing failure in producing a viable existential ethic. Kierkegaard's inner dynamic of ethicality was finally no more than a transposition of the externality of isolation into the structure of the self.

IDEALS IN MORAL REFLECTION

The structure of the psychological process of moral reflection has been called by Wollheim "one of the obscurest issues in human culture."[15] One of the major reasons for this obscurity, I believe, is that what is sought cannot be merely a description of the causal mechanisms involved. This is so for two reasons. First, what is desired is an 'internal' account, revelatory to the self of the structure of its own representations rather than those of the neuropsychologist. It may perhaps turn out that certain stages of the process, as they are in themselves, are impenetrable to the understanding of the self: structure is always ahead of representation. Nevertheless, we may still seek a theoretical representation of whatever understanding we *have* gained—not to gain control of a technology of moral motivation, but to broaden and deepen the web of humanistic concepts which constitute the common self-understanding of culture. Second, the reductionist inquiry into causal mechanisms avoids the question of the *rationality* of moral motivation. Recognition of this was, after all, a key motivation behind Kant's project to transpose the reflection on principle from the theoretical to the practical domain. Nevertheless, too much was thereby given up. An adequate account of moral rationality must extend beyond the internal coherence of the principle to include also the motivation to act on it as well. Such a project demands a theory of the self. Ethical life does not *begin* from the rationality of principle; even Kant's moral law itself, as Kant himself says, "begins at my invisible self."[16]

Another reason for the obscurity of the issue is that moral reflection also involves operations within the *unconscious dramaturgy*.[17] The 'as' of seeing-as points beyond the objectivities of principle and the particularities of circumstance to the original psychic structures of signification. Ethical seeing-as is halfway between 'derivable from a moral rule' and 'desired by the self.' (Whereas Kant, at least in his critical writings,[18] thought of these as an either/or.) As such, it draws upon a notion of good prior to that derived from reflection on moral principles and refers to processes internal to the structure of the self. Ethical ideals present themselves to the self in such a way that not seeking to forward them concretely would be tantamount to abandoning one's self—to a kind of death. In ethical imagination a special kind of concrete possibility is imagined for the self—one which traces back to the self's origins and identity, and traces back in a particular way. This gives to the self a moral autonomy which is not merely submission to principle and to ideals an authority which is not merely declaration or fiat. Ethics is not *merely* a project of conscious life, but a set of potent symbolic transactions in which the determinations of reason are mapped onto archaic unconscious dynamics through a web of metaphorical significations.[19]

The function of imagination in ethical idealization is to unite justification with motivation in such a way that the development of the self's maturity is forwarded. This places the work of imagination in the domain of a private ethical reflection, one which is sensitive to, but not reducible to, the arena of public criticism. It is a form of understanding which, at bottom, possesses its own autonomy. It is not primarily fictive in character (although it has elements of this), nor is it ethically neutral. Ethical idealization is not a matter of pretending or make-believe. It is a way of schematizing our world—cognitive, open to the tests of reality, and jointly operative with other modes of experience. It is shaped by cultural influences, but emerges as an autonomous form of thought through a purely private reflection of the individual consciousness. In this reflection, reason is not so much abandoned in favor of lawless imagining, but rather imagination enters into the space of reasons. The theory-practice opposition is maintained, but its center of balance is shifted so that it is not (as it is for Kant) the fulcrum of ethical rationality. Particularities of place, time, and circumstance form the matter of a concrete (rather than practical) ethical reflection in which ideals play a central role and in which imagination may be seen to be crucially cognitive.

In consequence, the ethical will be defined not solely in terms of the objects of that reflection but in term of its inner structure. It is within this structure that the imagination takes on its specifically ethical character. This 'ethicizing' of the imagination in ide-alization is not divorced from the activities of moral judgment and the extension of sympathy. Indeed, it enables us to see *why* these are the activities of an ethical person. It lifts sympathy out of the realm of the merely sentimental to a level that is recognizably ethical in its motivation, and it hones moral judgment to the level of ethical discernment.

The authoritative and motivational ground of ethical ideals is located in the degree to which the ideal or principle truly restores continuity and integrity to the developing self. Ethical idealization is the development, not primarily of a certain self-image that one strives to live up to, but of a certain self-structure. But this struc-ture is not merely a collection of self images. More essentially it is a set of ideational schemata in which reflection and ways of seeing one's environment interact. To be a self is to be a self-knower (not that the self is what one knows of oneself). In its ideals the self develops its schemata of interpretation in such a way that an alteration in the structure of the self (whether gradually or all of a sudden) is brought about.

CHAPTER 6

The Moral Philosophy of the Self

Two things fill the mind with ever new and increasing admiration
and awe, the oftener and more steadily we reflect on them: the
starry heavens above me and the moral law within me. . . . The
former begins at the place I occupy in the world of sense. . . . The
latter begins at my invisible self. . . . The former view of a countless
multitude of worlds annihilates, as it were, my importance as an
animal creature. . . . The latter, on the contrary, infinitely raises my
worth as that of an intelligence by my personality, in which the
moral law reveals a life independent of all animality and even of
the whole world of sense . . .

Kant, *Critique of Practical Reason*[1]

INTRODUCTION

Although the word *self* hardly appears with any consistent analysis in modern ethics, the history of the concept stretches back to
the beginning of Western moral theory. Plato's image in the
Republic[2] and the *Phaedrus*[3] of the good man as one who has
achieved self-mastery through ordering the three elements of the
soul—desire (or appetite), spirit (or noble ambition), and reason—has exerted powerful influence for millennia. But the psyche
is not the self in the sense of reflexive consciousness that has
obtained in modern philosophy since Descartes. The Greek word
psyche is much broader and has only loosely been translated as
mind, spirit, or soul. Also, according to Bremmer,[4] it often lacked
the connotations of individual psychology with which the modern
concept of self is usually enmeshed. Plato cannot therefore be rea-
sonably viewed as offering a theory of the self in a sense other
than offering a theory of the psyche (understood, loosely, as the
sum total of our mental apparatus).

The modern concept of self is elusive. In commonsense usage,
'self' is often used simply to mean the whole individual—body
and mind. Upon reflection, however, most of us would want to

modify this. Take the case of a soldier in battle who performs some heroic act at the cost of losing one of his legs. He has certainly lost part of his body, but we would be reluctant to say that, necessarily, his self has also been diminished. Intuitions of this sort have lain behind the tendency of philosophers (especially in the West) to identify the self with the mind rather than the body, particularly that part of the mind responsible for consciousness.[5] At the beginning of the modern period, Descartes defined the mind as an "I," a conscious substance, the subject of a reflexive self-awareness: "I am, I exist, is necessarily true each time that I pronounce it, or that I mentally conceive it."[6] But although the *cogito ergo sum* significantly shaped the epistemology of Western thought, the substantivity of the "I" as a mental substance, the *sum res cogitans*, met early resistance. Locke agreed that self was a conscious substance:

> *Self* is that conscious thinking thing whatever substance made up of, (whether spiritual or material, simple or compound, it matters not) which is sensible or conscious of pleasure and pain, capable of happiness or misery, and so is concerned for *itself*, as far as that consciousness extends.[7]

But he left the question of whether the self's substance was mental or physical, simple or compound, epistemologically open. What was important to Locke was the *identity* of the self (i.e., what was responsible for its continuity over time), and this could be shown to be memory. An amnesiac would be two selves, a reincarnated man would be one. Hume went further to attack the notions of identity and simplicity that Descartes had embedded in the concept of self:

> There are some philosophers, who imagine that we are every moment intimately conscious of what we call our SELF; that we feel its existence and continuation in existence; and are certain, beyond the evidence of a demonstration; both of its perfect identity and simplicity. . . . Unluckily all these positive assertions are contrary to that very experience, which is pleaded for them, nor have we any idea of *self*, after the manner it is here explain'd. For from what impression could this idea be derived?[8]

True to his skeptical starting points, Hume could not deny that it was possible that some people *did* have such a sense of self; he was sure only that *most* did not:

But setting aside some metaphysicians of this kind, I may venture to affirm of the rest of mankind, that they are nothing but a bundle or collection of different perceptions, which succeed each other with inconceivable rapidity, and are in a perpetual flux and movement. . . . The mind is a kind of theatre, where several perceptions successively make their appearance; pass, repass, glide away, and mingle in an infinite variety of postures and situations. There is properly no *simplicity* in it at one time, nor *identity* in it at different.[9]

Kant attempted to rescue the concept of the self by distinguishing between an empirical or *phenomenal* self and a *noumenal* or transcendental self.[10] Kant's doctrine of self-consciousness is, like his theory of imagination, one of the least transparent parts of his work. As Broad notes: "Kant's account of the nature of the human self and of its knowledge of itself is extremely complicated, and it is doubtful whether a single consistent doctrine can be extracted from his utterances."[11] In his critical view, Kant agreed with Hume that we could have no empirical knowledge of the self as it really is, but we could nevertheless have an a priori intuition of it as the formal condition of experience—i.e., in Broad's terms, "as a something which synthesizes data according to rules, in such a way as to produce the appearance of a self which persists through time and owns a number of experiences occurring at various dates and lasting for various periods."[12] As part of his 'Copernican revolution' in philosophy, Kant argued that Hume failed to see the connection between self-awareness and consciousness of objects. In order to know that my experience of some object is *my* experience, and not someone else's (and we *do* know this) we must presuppose a single self, an 'I think' which accompanies all our representations. This self is expressed in empirical consciousness (through a combination of the productive imagination and the faculty of understanding) as the sense that 'I am I.' (Kant calls this sense the synthetic unity of apperception.) But this empirical sense of self (under the subjectively imposed form of time), which he calls the *phenomenal* self, is distinguished from the transcendental, intelligible, *noumenal* self. The former is a representation only, and we can have no theoretical knowledge of the latter. It is a limit or negative concept only (like the concept of infinity—we cannot experience infinity). We can only have practical knowledge of it in moral action (i.e., actions in which we act on maxims derived from inner laws which we freely make for ourselves *insofar as* we are rational beings). For Kant, a rational psychology of the noumenal self is impossible. We must assume it as the unity of our consciousness, but beyond that we can have no positive theoretical knowledge of it. Practically, however, we can know our free and rational unity as the precondition of moral action. Kant's analysis of the self, then, bequeathed a double mystery to moral philosophy. The self which is the center of moral action is completely unknowable by reason, and yet the requisite self-certainty is nevertheless still possible through a mysterious 'practical knowledge' (which by definition must include no element of theoretical understanding).

THE SELF IN MORAL LIFE

It would take us too far afield to trace the vicissitudes of the concept of the self through the development of modern philosophy. Charles Taylor, in *Sources of the Self*,[13] has already performed this task comprehensively in his masterly portrait of modern self-identity, detailing the profound rifts which exist in its moral sources. We can simply say at this point that, without an adequate theory of the self, moral philosophy lacks the ideal of a whole human being. And whatever else moral life is, it must ultimately engage our whole person.

Ethics is the domain of right relations between persons insofar as they are persons. A person is an embodied self; selfhood is the inward dimension of persons. The three constitutive features of selfhood are rationality, freedom of choice and thought, and self-consciousness. Human selfhood being what it is, moral life between persons can be defined in terms of relations of respect, responsibility, and concern for the dignity, welfare, and happiness of persons. To speak of persons as 'embodied selves' is not to embrace a Cartesian dualism of body and mind. It is simply to say that persons have an inward and outward aspect, both of which must be taken into account in our moral life. Whether selves can exist without bodies is a religious question, not a philosophical one. Moral philosophy must deal with persons in toto. But the inward dimension of persons *can* nevertheless be studied by rational methods—namely, through an adequate psychology of the self.

Each of these three moral relations between persons—*respect*, *responsibility*, and *concern*—need some elaboration. Kant, the preeminent philosopher of respect, distinguished (I think rightly) between two kind of value, dignity and price:

> In the realm of ends, everything has either a *price* or a *dignity*. Whatever has a price can be replaced by something else as its equivalent; on the other hand, whatever is above all price, and therefore admits of no equivalent, has a dignity. . . . An end in itself does not have mere relative worth, i.e., a price, but an intrinsic worth, i.e., *dignity*.[14]

Price is the relative value a thing has as a means to an end—its exchange value. Dignity is value that is absolute in the sense that it cannot be exchanged for something equivalent: there *is* no equivalent. Only persons have dignity. Dignity is the value that persons have as selves. Respect, therefore, is the recognition that a being has value beyond mere price (exchange value). In other words, respect is the recognition of dignity.

Kant goes on, of course, to say that dignity is intrinsic value: a universal, innate, overriding, and independent value of persons as such. I tend to agree, although I am uncertain that this additional interpretation is a necessary feature of ethical ideals; it may just be a feature of some Western styles of moral reflection. Certainly the notion of intrinsic worth is not common to all moral systems, and many people seem to live very moral lives without it. Alternative concepts of dignity can do a great deal of the moral work that Kant's does. Two in particular stand out. The first is dignity as an individual achievement, which gives one a publicly recognized stature of reputation, prestige, position, and honor. In this view, dignity is an earned entitlement to respect because of an individual's past performance. Such a concept finds a clear place in warrior and mercantile ethics and would be defined through the possession of certain virtues. This is the notion of dignity favored by Hobbes: "The value, or worth, of a man, is as of all other things, his price; that is to say, as much as would be given for the use of his power; and, therefore not absolute, but a thing dependent on the need and judgment of another. . . . The public worth of a man, which is the value set on him by the Commonwealth, is that which men commonly call *dignity*."[15]

The second concept defines dignity as self-respect or self-esteem—the conscious sense of self worth of an individual. Moral self-respect would involve the valuing of one's character in a way that did justice to oneself as a free, rational, and self-conscious being. This virtue is obviously crucial to the development of moral life in an individual, although it is rather obscure as a guide in one's relations with others. Neither of these latter notions treat dignity as universally possessed by all human beings. I believe they are therefore morally limited, although this would be a hard thing to prove.

Kant is the great philosopher of respect, although the feature of persons that drew his respect was their capacity to freely follow rational moral laws;   their concrete personhood did not capture his philosophical imagination. Because he lived at a time in which an adequate psychological theory with which to map the structure of ethical self-reflection was missing, he assimilated the rationality of that reflection (of which he was so exquisitely aware) to the ideal of rationality afforded by the physical sciences. He was in no doubt that this severed rational links between understanding and motivation:

> The understanding . . . can judge, but to give to this judgment of the understanding a compelling force, to make it an incentive that can move the will to perform the action—this is the philosopher's stone![16]

The result was an ethical theory which, subjectively, treated morality as submission to principles external to the desires of the concrete self. This was surely a precursor to the theory of repression, later to be developed by Freudian thought as the origination of morality in oedipal guilt. To be sure, a morality grounded solely in principles has a number of psychological benefits in undercutting delusive attempts at disguising self-concern as concern for other. But too strong an attachment to the notion of principle may lead, not to psychological maturity, but to subtly dangerous forms of self-deception, to claims of substantive objectivity which lead in turn to covert or overt compulsion, in the name of moral truth, of others following different ideals. This point can easily be misunderstood. There are two things that I am specifically *not* saying. I am not saying that compulsion is not sometimes practically necessary and appropriate (e.g., in cases of adult sociopathic behavior and at certain points in childrearing). Nor am I saying that all ideals are ethically equal from either an individual or a social point of view. Some ideals are higher, profounder, more attuned to the needs of the world and the needs of the self than others. This is true and can be seen to be true by all who are committed to rational inquiry into the matter. Some ideals ought actively to be resisted (because, for example, they are confused at levels deeper than those who advocate them are aware of and will have consequences other than what their advocates believe that they will have). The point is that such resistance and compulsion cannot be pursued in the name of a universal truth of the matter.

Responsibility is the attitude of intentionality (reflective purposiveness) and accountability (willingness to answer for one's conduct) regarding one's life and actions. *Moral* responsibility is intentionality and accountability for the dignity, welfare, and happiness of persons. Intentionality is the attitude of mind in which one formulates the reasons and purposes for which one acts; it forms the basis for the concept of agency. Full moral agency requires a strong sense of intentionality, one in which the self is intimately involved in its reasons and purposes. Beings that are not selves (computers, androids, corporations) cannot therefore be full moral agents. Responsibility also requires accountability; a moral life is hardly possible without some acknowledgement of one's commitments, recognition of one's obligations, and culpability for one's actions. The accountability required for responsibility may be purely internal (i.e., accountability to one's conscience—one's reflective sense of right and wrong), or it may include public forms of accountability as well. External accountability about some things is necessary for a healthy society. But internal accountability is the heart and soul of morality. It is the expression of the self's autonomy, in which it claims *ownership* of its life and actions.

Accountability presupposes causality, the ability to make something happen. Ought implies can. But there are two senses of causality that moral life must be concerned with—agent causality and structural causality. Agent causality is a relationship between a particular person and a range of actions. Persons can also exercise causality, however, even without performing actions, both by possessing a certain self-structure and by belonging to specific social structures.[17] Structural causality determines a relationship between persons simply by its existence. This is why one is responsible for the kind of person that one *is* rather than merely for what one *does*. Structural causality refers to any area over which one exercises power and authority. You can rightly be blamed for something even if you did not directly cause it simply by participating in a structure which has brought that thing about.

Part of responsibility is the recognition of obligation: something owed or due: L. *obligare: ob* (to) + *ligare* (to bind) to do. A duty is an obligation given content by a context (circumstance plus relevant values). There is a strong temptation to formulate these relevant values in principles, particularly when the values are almost universally acknowledged to be overridingly good: don't lie, don't hurt people, be kind to others, and so on. And doing so helps to organize much of our moral life efficiently, as well as aiding in moral education. But if the principles are so central to our moral life, it is only because they express, more or less precisely, values of respect, responsibility, and concern that the self cannot well do without in its ongoing process of growth, integration, and restoration. The prescriptive character of such principles, their *oughtness*, is simply an expression of this acknowledged commitment. Ultimately, duties are derived from values, not principles, and they always trace their paths of moral authority from relationships between one's self-structure and particular individuals.

In addition to obligation, the domain of responsibility also includes the supererogatory (L. *supererogatus*, beyond the call of duty). The ethics of principle draws a sharp line between duty and the supererogatory, but the value-based ethics of ideals treats this as a matter of degree. Traditionally, supererogatory acts are treated as acts of charity or philanthropy, acts for which we may be praised if we perform them, but not blamed if we do not. The ethics of ideals holds us fully accountable (subject to both praise and blame) by our conscience even for supererogatory acts. Although it reduces the number of moral duties that we may feel, it increases the number of things for which we are responsible (e.g., contributing to the end of world hunger). Both duties and the supererogatory are called forth from the same sources in the self, our understanding of moral value which is established ultimately by our ideals. In reality, the line between duties and the supererogatory is artificial, a matter of distinguishing the morally urgent from that which is less so.

Responsibility is to many people a puzzling notion because it seems to be at the same time a matter of free choice and something that is thrust on us by our situation, regardless of our wants or desires. How can we be both free and responsible? The answer of the ethics of ideals is in one way the same as Kant's ethics. It is to distinguish between two senses of freedom, negative and positive (i.e., autonomy), with the latter being the mark of ethical life. Negative freedom is freedom from external constraint in the pursuit of our desires or ambitions. Positive freedom, or autonomy, is the ability to be guided and led in our life by ends that are truly the self's own. The difference, of course, is that these ends are now treated as ideals rather than principles, and that what is regarded as one's own is not determined by reason per se, but by the degree to which the self has achieved wholeness in its relations with others.

Concern or care is a psychological attitude of loving and sympathetic interest in the welfare of others. More than the other features of ethical ideals, it engages the emotional side of human beings, the side in which the meanings of the world are felt rather than judged. Concern brings perceived moral realities home to our most vulnerable center, and is the source of some of our grandest ideals. Concern is at the heart of the utilitarian emphasis on sympathy and the general happiness. Some feminists, such as Carol Gilligan,[18] have argued that because women are more loving, sympathetic, and emotional than men, care is a particular moral strength of women. This undoubtedly has some broad historical justification, and this is one of the things that men admire about women. It is doubtful, however, that it can constitute a separate ethic. Without adequate psychological connection to respect and responsibility, concern can diffuse into sentimentalism, bias, and an unwillingness to undertake responsibilities which do not engage our sympathies. A more likely account of gender differences in moral personality would treat the relative presence of respect, responsibility, and concern as a very loose variation of spread between both men and women.

It may be objected that this threefold view of moral life has as a consequence that two persons in a single situation, having conflicting ideals guiding their actions, might be equally ethical. And this is quite true. Owen Flanagan has shown how different psychological structures can produce a wide variety of different but equally autonomous moral personalities.[19] But a good part of the concern here misses the point. The objection assumes that the ethical can only be understood objectively—i.e., in terms of which objects the self concerns itself with, and which relationships (expressed in principles) between those objects the self endorses. And because these objects may be related in conflicting ways, contrary ways of relating them cannot be considered equally ethical.

But it is precisely this limitation of ethical thought to a reflection on principle that is being called into question here. The subjective dimension of the ethical (i.e., that which is to be understood in terms of a characterization of the structure of the self) *does* permit the possibility that contrary schematizations of a situation may be equally ethical. This is not to say that contrary schematizations are equally well-thought-out in terms of consequences. Nor is it to say, of course, that all contrary schematization *are* of equal ethical worth, only that *some might* be. The logic of right is different here: unlike principles, ideals are not fundamentally imperative. They both motivate and justify the self by directing desire through a psycho-symbolic translation code which interprets the action cues (the aspects attended to in the seeing-as schema) in a perceived situation in the direction of a good which the self experiences (at some level) as constitutive of its identity. Right is one's way to the good.

Clearly moral philosophy needs a sophisticated and substantive theory of the self—one that relates the structural features of consciousness, identity, and reflexivity to the substantive ends that we pursue and the situations within which we find ourselves. But it was not until the rise of psychoanalysis (beginning with Freud's classical tripartite model of id, ego, and superego) that this began to be possible. The next section is devoted to an examination of two psychoanalytic approaches which have provided us with concepts of self and idealization more densely elaborated than those available to Kant and Kierkegaard—the classical tradition originating with Freud, and the self psychology of Heinz Kohut. Freudian theory locates the origination of idealization in a derivation from idealized objects or in the modification of drives according to the pleasure principle. For Kohut, ideals are *part of the self*, deriving from the self's original identity in the self: selfobject matrix, and arriving at the true object choice of autonomous structures of the self through a gradual decathexis of narcissistically experienced archaic objects.

PART 2

Imagination in Ethics: Psychological Aspects

CHAPTER 7

The Self in Classical Psychoanalysis

> Who today can still say that his anger is really his own anger with so many people butting in and knowing so much more about it than he does? There has arisen a world of qualities without a man to them, of experiences without anyone to experience them, and it almost looks as though under ideal conditions man would no longer experience anything at all, and the comforting weight of personal responsibility would dissolve into a system of formulae for potential meanings.
>
> Robert Musil, *The Man Without Qualities*[1]

As psychodynamic processes, ethical ideals require placement within a psychology that explains their origin, their structural relations to other parts of the self, and their connection with cognitive and motivational processes. Presently, however, the concept of the self in psychoanalytic theory is the subject of vigorous debate.[2] From its relatively obscure place in traditional Freudian theory, it has emerged as a central theme of debates between several major schools. It would not be too much to say that, today, the concept of the self lies at the heart of opposing conceptions of psychoanalytic practice.

By classical psychoanalysis, I mean the tradition which began with Freud's tripartite division of the person into unconscious, preconscious, and conscious systems between 1900 and 1923, and id, ego, and superego thereafter. Classical psychoanalysis has been ambivalent, to say the least, about the concept of the self. Discussion has been marked by terminological confusion at several levels. The term *self* has been used as a *systemic* concept to refer in general to the intrapsychic systems of id, ego, and superego taken in toto, although it has also been equated with the subsystem of the ego, or a part of that subsystem. It has been used in a *structural* sense to refer to the structure of drives and defenses, discharges, restraints, and associations organized around the intrapsychic systems.[3] The structural sense distinguished the self both as agent and as object of scientific study. *Self* has also been used in a *representational* sense to express the experiential elements of the 'I,' or some narrower set of representational elements within reflective experience—usually seen in terms of a fantasy product or deceptive self-images.[4] The representational concept enabled the self to be placed as a nexus in a sociocultural environment and as introspective self-experiencer.

Significant distinctions have also emerged between the ego as a psychic system and the interpersonal self in its object relations. The ongoing contributions of the British school of object-relations theory (principally supplying representational concepts) and the American school of ego psychology (principally supplying structural concepts) add a further complexity to the issue, even though their focus is not primarily the concept of the self.[5] Finally, somatic aspects have at times been incorporated into the concept to distinguish in a broad way between the body-mind as subject and its world.[6]

Part of the reason for this plethora of meanings within the classical tradition is traceable to ambiguities within Freud's own thought. Freud's own use of the term *das Ich* underwent a gradual modification over the years. In his 1914 paper "On Narcissism," he used the term to refer to the self in a loose superordinate sense as the person in general. But experiential and non-systemic concepts of the self did not fit well with Freud's goal of establishing psychoanalysis on the firm foundation of nineteenth-century science. Indeed, as early as 1897, Freud rejected the possibility of unmediated self-knowledge: "My self-analysis is still interrupted. I have now seen why. I can only analyse myself with objectively acquired knowledge (as if I were a stranger); self-analysis is really impossible, otherwise there would be no illness."[7]

In his editorial introduction to Freud's *The Ego and the Id* (1923), Strachey points out that it "seems possible to detect two main uses: one in which the term distinguishes a person's self as a whole . . . from other people, and the other in which it denotes a particular part of the mind characterized by special attributes and functions."[8] Except for a very few cases, Strachey translated *das Ich* as 'ego,' rather than 'I' or 'self.' This editorial decision had significant consequences for the development of classical psychoanalysis in the English-speaking world, as 'ego' connotated a more impersonal and relatively intrapsychic concept, thus inhibiting for some time the investigation of the experiential and inter-personal aspects of the self.[9] In the development of classical psy-choanalysis, structural and systemic concepts of the self tended to predominate, with representational concepts gradually being absorbed into the theory of object relations and superordinate concepts being relegated to the commonsense (i.e., nonscientific) level. The early ambiguity disappeared.[10]

During the 1950s, the distinction for classical psychoanalysis between self and ego became clarified in the ego psychology of Heinz Hartmann.[11] The ego was identified as a systemic entity within the tripartite system, while the self as a whole was treated as an object of inner association or representation (a 'me' rather than and 'I'). Hartman later elaborated this distinction in terms of a distinction between structural and representational concepts of the self and defined the self in terms of object relations as the sub-jective personal dimension; hence, object cathexis (i.e., psycholog-ical investment, including that form know as narcissism) was no longer treated as a cathexis of the ego, but as a cathexis of the self.[12] Hartman's somewhat forced distinction between ego and self turned the latter into something of an orphan concept, its clinical and metapsychological aspects being treated under the concepts of self-image, self-representation, and so on. This effec-tively removed the self from serious psychoanalytic study, while creating an explanatory lacuna in the attempt to understand the structural, experiential, and descriptive aspects of ego function-ing. The morally crucial notions of character structure and subjec-tive consciousness could gain no foothold. Even after Hartmann had distinguished self from ego, ambiguities remained. Hartmann generally used 'self' to refer to the subjective life of the whole per-son in both its bodily and psychic activities. But at the same time he treats it as the intrapsychic aggregate of self-representations, which would make the self a subcategory of the ego's representa-tional function. The question of what part the self plays in the intrapsychic economy—structural or representational—is left unanswered.[13]

During the 1960s, some psychoanalysts working within the classical tripartite model of psychic activity strove to resuscitate the representational model of the self, hoping that a more sophis-ticated approach to representation would be able to incorporate the self's more structural dimensions of subjectivity and agency. Spiegel,[14] for example, defined the self as a "pooling and averaging" of the cathexes of individual self-representations. He distinguished the intrapsychic self from person as "psyche" and "soma" and further distinguishes the self from individual self-representations (which he treated as individual memory images of the body and its functions cathected with narcissistic libido).

This approach was continued in the work of Joseph Sandler and his associates, who sought to understand the self in terms of its representational world.[15] The phenomena of introjection and identification[16] were not well accounted for by purely intrasystemic concepts. Individuals, they argued, possess affectively structured representations of ideal states which involve a particualr self-representation and certain relation to the world of objects. The ego is the bearer of these affectively charged desired states, as well as of the fantasies which perpetuate them. The ego functions to compare these ideal states with the "perceived state." In pathological conditions, this reality testing may be severely impaired. On this view, while ego is a systemic concept, self is a representational concept. Nevertheless, both object relations and the representational world remained functions of the ego.

Recently, Otto Kernberg has systematically expanded the representational and object-relations role of the self within the tripartite system. Kernberg makes the large theoretical claim that "the self-object-affect units are primary determinants of the overall structures of the mind,[17] and goes so far as to argue that affects rather than drives are the essential motivational force in psychic development. For Kernberg, the self is a substructure of the ego with affective and cognitive components, derived from forerunners in the ego that predate the integration of the tripartite structure.[18] These forerunners of the self are early self-representations arising at first in the undifferentiated symbiotic phase of mother-infant ineraction. As these representations become libidinally and aggressively cathected, they evolve into a substructure of the ego.

Kernberg's work and the work of other representational and object-relations theorists (it seems to me) offers the most promising line within classical psychoanalysis for a theory of mature moral development. The narrowly interpreted systemic model leaves little room for morality as other than a series of superego prohibitions, external to the 'I', internalized from parental figures. Representational concepts of the self offer several advantages over the cumbersome metaphors of an 'inner' and 'outer' world resorted to by the systemic model, particularly in explaining psychological investment (cathexis).[19] Also, they seem better able to account for features of self-experience and the more integrated aspects of personhood.

Yet the combination of represenational, structural, systemic, and object-relations concepts within the classical tripartite model is an uneasy alliance. Classical psychoanalysis is faced with two intersecting problems in its treatment of the self. The first is the problem of finding appropriate bridge concepts between the structural concepts of classical psychoanalysis and the new representational concepts. The second is the problem of the place of self-representations in self-identity. It is clear that the internalization transactions between child and parent cannot be excluded from a structural account of psychic activity. Nevertheless, as a representation, self-organization does not play a structural role in motivational dynamics. It cannot be an agent. Sandler himself speaks of introjects having "demands and standards."[20] More structurally oriented analysts have objected that this is a confusion of frames of reference, attempting to make representational concepts do the work of structural ones: "But an image in the mind cannot do anything."[21] The relationship between representational concepts and structural concepts is a complex one that is not disposed of by easy metaphors, such as that the self-representation is *contained* in the ego. Structure and representation cannot be treated as two words for the same thing.

Boesky has argued that Kernberg's elevation of self-representations and object-representations to the level of organizing structures largely ignores the role of unconscious fantasy in this organizing system and conflicts with clinical data on the structural aspects of introjection.[22] Regardless of theoretical decisions about the role of representations, clinical evidence reveals that a good part of identity is determined by structural processes of conflict, compromise formation, and unconscious fantasy. In addition, there is more to self-identity than modifications of self-representation in the system ego. The problem of explicating narcissism—with its cathexes of libido and/or aggression—becomes particularly difficult on representational assumptions.

Meissner, although more sympathetic than Boesky to the need for a theory of the self in psychoanalysis, argues that Kernberg glosses over problems in the representational vs. structural debate.[23] Are id, ego, and superego now nonself? How does the self take on ego function? Also, what is a self-representation a representation of? According to Meissner, although the systemic[24] model of classical psychoanalysis leaves little room for integrated self-experience and hence no room for autonomous action, representational additions to that model do not seem to add any workable theory. We need a concept that shows how self-awareness can itself be a source of psychic activity. Although he does not support Kohut's views (especially Kohut's theory of narcissism), Meissner argues that a notion of self, rather than the ego, as a center of object relations generates a phenomenologically richer view of the internalization processes of introjection and identification.

In conclusion we can say that, despite creative expansions by later classical psychoanalysts, Freud's original systemic framework has proved too constrictive to contain the self-concepts necessary to explain the facts of both identity formation and internalization in the self-object matrix. Further development in these areas (e.g., the work of George Klein[25] and Gedo[26]) has repeatedly demonstrated the need to move outside the tripartite model. Nowhere is this more evident than in the moral psychology of ideals to which we now turn.

CHAPTER 8

Ethical Idealization in Classical Psychoanalysis

[R]ight is the might of a community. It is still violence, ready to be directed against any individual who resists it; it works by the same methods and follows the same purposes. The only real difference lies in the fact that what prevails is no longer the violence of an individual but that of a community.

Sigmund Freud, *letter to Einstein*[1]

FREUD

Three preliminary difficulties face us in trying to locate the theoretical position of the concept of idealization within Freud's tripartite psychic system. First, Freud himself did not develop a specific theory of idealization. He frequently (and not always consistently) used the terms "ideal," "ego ideal," and "idealization" in his attempt to understand the ego and its libido, but his remarks on idealization are scattered through his writings and receive no sustained treatment. Second, as his concept of the ego ideal became more clearly defined as the superego, the idealizing aspects of this psychic subsystem gradually become displaced by more prohibitional concepts in that area of his thought. Third, Freud tended to speak of idealization in two ways: first from the point of view of his original drive-defense model in which it was understood as a reactive product of early childhood experiences; and second from his developing theory of object relations which he was attempting to subsume under that model (in which it was understood as a fantasy product which needs to be countered by a reality principle). Historically, despite some early vacillation, it is the former concept which came to be incorporated into classical moral psychology.[2]

Both approaches, however, are grounded in Freud's theory of

narcissism. In his early essay, "On Narcissism" (1914),[3] written before he had developed the systemic model, Freud's primary drive concepts were that of libido and the ego instincts (consisting of both self-preservation drives and the agency of repression). His theory of narcissism aimed to show how narcissistic libido was transformed into object libido: as objects became distinguished from the ego (self), erotic libidinal drives (e.g., for the breast) could become "attached" to the ego instincts (e.g., the hunger drive). But some "overflow" of narcissistic libido into the object also occurred to form the basis of choice of "love" objects. Freud spoke of this as "idealization" although he provided little integration of this concept with his drive theory:

> Being in love consists in a flowing over of ego libido into the object. It has the power to remove repressions and re-instate perversions. It exalts the sexual object into a sexual ideal. Since, with the object type (or attachment type), being in love occurs in virtue of the fulfillment of infantile conditions for loving, we may say that whatever fulfills that condition is idealized.[4]

Freud elaborated a few years later:

> The tendency which falsifies judgment in this respect [being in love] is that of *idealization*. But now it is easier for us to find our bearings. We see that the object is being treated in the same way as our own ego, so that when we are in love a considerable amount of narcissistic libido overflows on to the object. It is even obvious, in many forms of love-choice, that the object serves as a substitute for some unattained ego ideal of our own. We love it on account of the perfections which we have striven to reach for our own ego, and which we should now like to procure in this roundabout way as a means of satisfaction of our narcissism.[5]

At the same time, and not easily compatible with his model of energic overflow,[6] Freud developed a notion of idealization based on self-object relations but still within the boundaries of his theory of narcissism. This form of idealization results from the internalization of parental objects. He called this "anaclitic object choice" (from the Greek word *anaklinein*, "to lean upon"). In this sense, idealization for Freud became synonymous with overvaluation of the object. The object enjoys a considerable degree of freedom from criticism, its qualities are comparatively magnified, and reality testing becomes more casual.

It is somewhat unclear why Freud felt the need for two theories of object idealization. Spruiell[7] has speculated that it stems from his interest in characterizing the differences in the ways that men and women love other persons—men (according to Freud) tending to make anaclitic choices and women tending to make narcissistic ones. But his treatment of idealization in terms of object relations is important because it serves (along with narcissistic investment) as a major source for Freud's concept of the ego ideal or superego, which in turn (as we shall see) forms the core of his understanding of the role of idealization in moral life. This dual origin of the superego led to a number of conceptual ambiguities which continue today to be a source of debate and confusion in classical psychoanalysis.

Also in "On Narcissism,"[8] Freud first introduces the term *ego ideal* as a product of infantile narcissism. As a result of the intrusion of reality onto narcissistic enjoyment and the corresponding need to submit to external standards and regulation, a normally developing person does not abandon his narcissism but displaces it. The self-love that was enjoyed in childhood by the actual ego is transferred to the ideal ego, to which every perfection is attributed. The ideal ego "is the substitute for the lost narcissism of his childhood when he was his own ideal."[9] In this early essay, Freud distinguishes between the narcissistic ego ideal and the institution of conscience, the latter deriving from the internalization of parental objects). This distinction is more or less maintained in the *Introductory Lectures* (1916–17). But in 1921, in *Group Psychology and the Analysis of the Ego*, Freud assimilates the ego ideal into the agency of conscience. In "The Ego and the Id" (1923),[10] where Freud first clearly articulates his tripartite model of the psyche, he identifies the ego ideal with the superego, expressing a preference (later to be institutionalized) for the latter term. The punitive and critical functions begin to overshadow the original emphasis on narcissistic satisfaction.[11] In addition, the roots of the ego ideal in identifications with both mother and father, as well as the centrality of the Oedipus complex in the formation of the ego ideal–superego, began to be formulated: "The ego ideal, therefore, is the heir of the Oedipus complex, and thus it is also the expression of the most powerful impulses and most important vicissitudes experienced by the libido in the id."[12] Few other references to the ego ideal occur in Freud's writings. Freud thus presents us with a choice in the interpretation of idealization,

neither of which seem promising as a psychological framework
for the concept for mature moral ideals: it is either an undeveloped relic of infantile narcissism, or it is identical to the punitive
and prohibiting superego.

LATER DEVELOPMENTS IN
CLASSICAL PSYCHOANALYSIS

Several later analysts within the classical tradition have attempted
to reinstate a distinction between the functions of the ego-ideal
and the superego, drawing on Freud's early work on narcissism.
The motivation behind this reinstatement seem to have been,
principally, a greater sensitivity to internalization processes due to
the growing influence of British object-relations theory, the need
to resolve a significant ambiguity in Freudian thought, and a sense
(by some, at least) that the more positive elements of parental
influence had not been adequately incorporated into classical
developmental theory.

Nunberg (1932)[13] distinguishes the ego ideal as "an image of
the loved objects in the ego" which is absorbed by the ego and
cathected with the libido. The superego, however, is "an image of
the hated and feared objects" submitted to out of fear of punishment. Annie Reich (1954)[14] saw both as a result of ego identifications, but, whereas the ego ideal is based on early childhood
"identifications with parental figures seen in a glorified light,"
those of the superego are later "identifications resulting from the
breakdown of the Oedipus complex." Jacobson (1954)[15] sees the
ego ideal as a mediating process between the magical self-images
of childhood and the parental prohibitions of the superego, stemming from the desire to become one with the love object. Piers
and Singer (1953)[16] relate the distinction between superego and
ego ideal to the distinction between shame and guilt. The superego sets *boundaries* for the ego, the ego ideal sets *goals*. The ego
ideal represents the sum of positive identifications with the
parental images and stems (following the early Freud) from original narcissistic omnipotence. Guilt is a painful internal tension
which arises when the id impulses of aggression and sexuality
transgress the emotionally charged barriers set up by the superego. Shame arises when a goal of the ego ideal is not attained. The
psychological danger which prompts guilt is that of dismember-

ment and annihilation. The danger which produces shame is that of abandonment and rejection.

In general, classical psychoanalysis begins from this point to accept a distinction between ego ideal functions and the superego, but no longer strives to connect the ego ideal with moral values. Lample-de-Groot (1962)[17] clearly distinguishes the superego as the restrictive and prohibitive agency equivalent to conscience, while the ego ideal is a functionally independent need satisfying agency. The superego contains the 'ought' of parental demands, while the ego ideal relieves anxiety by providing assurance of fundamental identification with the omnipotent parents, acquiring its conative force through the conversion of object libido. This results in projective idealizing identifications with parental figures and their surrogates.

In the classical tradition, then, the ego ideal (insofar as it is distinguished from the superego) continued to be interpreted as either a product of infantile narcissism or as the set of positive identifications within the superego system stemming from the internalization of parental objects. Even in the latter case, however, it remains within the conflicted moral dynamics of parental identification, the Oedipus complex, and sexual guilt. In neither of these roles does the ego ideal participate in free and authentic ethical valuation. The psychodynamics of the ego ideal owe their conative force to a narcissistic cathexis derived from the conversion of object libido. The self is measured against not-self (the self I want to be, the ego ideal, the internalized parental imago) and found wanting. Classical psychoanalysis is thrown back on a systemic and inevitably conflicted concept of self as the compromised collection of id, ego, and superego.

HARTMANN'S EGO PSYCHOLOGY

A significant exception to this separation of idealization from moral valuation is offered by ego psychology. In 1962, Hartmann and Lowenstein[18] elaborated the ego ideal, not as a separate system to the superego but as one of its internal functions (alongside that of criticism and conscience)—namely that of holding up to the ego positive ideals which are the "correlates" of the taboos. Together, taboos plus ideals constitute the "superego system." The aggrandized self and overvalued self continue to be transformed even beyond the oedipal period. Taboos and ideal aims gradually become integrated to form a moral system. Although not all classical analysts agree with all that Hartmann says about the superego (Sandler and Novey,[19] for instance, believe that he has loaded too many functions into it), his study of the connections between superego and ego ideal have become widely accepted by those classical psychoanalysts who wish to allow a constructive role in moral psychology for the positive contents of the ego ideal.

Hartmann's approach grants some degree of *autonomy* to moral valuation. It gives a psychoanalytic description of the motivational dynamics through which an individual comes to distinguish in a rational way his or her *good* and *ought* from his or her *bad* and *ought not*. The ego ideal is no longer merely an agent of wishful thinking but a strategy of the ego, and it is relatively independent of both the drives and infantile object choice. Moreover, some substantive content can be given to these valuations by examining the specifics of the moral code which is transmitted through socialization processes and parental criticism. However, precisely because the rationality involved is the work of a subsystem of the self rather than the whole self, Hartmann can give no explanation of why the moral system as a whole has motivational authority for the reflective consciousness. The ego can determine which ideal ends are inconsistent with one another and which psychological means are suitable to accomplish those ends, but it cannot evaluate the rationality of the ends themselves. In *Psychoanalysis and Moral Values* (1960), one of the most serious attempts by classical psychoanalysis to grapple with the rationality of moral values, Hartmann says:

> Moral values may or may not agree with the code of the person who holds them, or with the prevalent codes of a given society, or with my own, the observer's code. In this there is nothing that would give us the right to apply the terms "true" or "false." What we state is only agreement or disagreement with a given code.[20]

One of Hartmann's chief concerns in this work is to answer the charge that Freudian moral psychology falls into an unhealthy kind of moral relativism by failing to make any discrimination between moral ends. Yet his account is bound by the same limits as other classical psychoanalytic accounts of idealization. We can distinguish, says Hartmann, between genuine and non-genuine valuations based on a self-scrutiny which is a function of the ego. But beyond this, the question of which values we *ought* to adopt or accept is a "decision," which therefore lies outside the boundaries of "empirical science." This does not mean that moral values are arbitrary, because "a person's moral behavior is as much an essential part and a distinctive sign of his personality as is his character or his instinctual life."[21] But the non-arbitrariness of moral values in this sense is not the non-arbitrariness that someone seeking moral wisdom would seek. Hitler's moral values are certainly non-arbitrary in the sense that they could be explained as part of his character, but we would still want to know why a choice between the value systems of Hitler and Albert Schweitzer is non-arbitrary.

Hartmann quite rightly points out that a good therapist will "concentrate on the realization of one category of values only: health values" (p. 55). Yet, although he is aware of the overlap between health values and moral values, he believes a clinical separation can be made precisely because, in his view (as in classical psychoanalysis generally), morals are social whereas psychological health is individual. What rational account can we give of the link between the adaptive desiderata of mental health and the prescriptive desiderata of moral values? What reasons (other than strategic) could a psychologically sophisticated person give for obeying the dictates of the superego when it conflicts with self-interest? Hartmann rejects the answer 'none' as a distortion of psychanalytic health values. Health values can determine which codes are incapable of being taken up as one's own due to their incompatibility with one's psychological history. They can determine which individual codes will be incompatible with widespread social codes (e.g., prohibitions against murder, unlimited lying and stealing, cannibalism as a regular practice, and abandonment of aged parents by children). And health values can rationally evaluate the internal consistency of an individual's moral code.

Despite his intentions, however, Hartmann fails to provide a notion of moral life which is both autonomous and rational. He vacillates between these but does not integrate them. His model of psychoanalysis as science requires that the rational reflection that is furthered by analysis *must* stop short of the values which are most deeply the self's own—its ideal ends. The idealization

process that gives these ends their autonomy excludes their rationality, thereby rendering their authority for reflective consciousness null.

Hartmann quite rightly points out that the analytic process
has limitations in the changes it can bring about in the analysand.
The analyst is not the patient and cannot do his restorative work
for him. But it is quite clear that Hartmann is doing more than
humbly restricting the scope of psychoanalysis. He is defining the
boundaries of rational discourse about values. With Freud, he is
convinced that, once we leave the borders of (classical) analysis,
we are in the domain of the arbitrary. If we ask the pointed question of *why* the rationality that is embodied in interactive analysis
cannot be applied, in principle, to ethical reflection within the
structure of the individual, we find in classical analysis not merely
an epistemological commitment to a certain kind of method, but
also a metaphysical commitment to a certain view of human
nature. It is not merely that rational understanding is limited in its
power to illuminate for the self the deepest springs of desire but,
more fundamentally (in line with Freudian beliefs about human
nature), what *is* illuminated will brutely resist transformation in
the direction of ethical ideals.

> There is a tendency easily recognizable in some civilizations . . .
> which would deny not only in oneself but also in mankind what
> would be deemed "radically bad." Thus with many persons for
> whom the idea of God persists, the idea of the devil has van-
> ished. Whatever the reasons for this development, the result has
> been a degree of optimism concerning the nature of man against
> which Freud has often warned—and which many of us, too,
> would judge ill-considered. (p. 94)

With this metaphysics of human nature, we have reached the
limits of Hartmann's ego psychology. It stems from the same
genealogy of morals as Freud's pessimistic comment to Einstein
quoted at the beginning of this chapter. Morality is the community's violence against the self. Hartmann may be less sanguine
than Freud about the split between reason and moral value, but
he remains committed to the same psychological model in which
that split is axiomatic. Rational self-understanding can prioritize
the substantive ends that we happen to have, it can rule out the
clearly irrational, and it can make some accommodation with
conditions. Rationality can operate in the space *between* desire

and its object, but it has no function within the structure of desire. In *The Future of an Illusion*, Freud says:

> In reality, there is no such thing as "eradicating" evil tendencies. . . . The inmost essence of human nature consists of elemental instincts, which are common to all men. . . . These instincts in themselves are neither good nor evil. We but classify them and their manifestations in that fashion, according as they meet the needs and demands of the human community.[22]

Such a moral psychology, notwithstanding protests to the contrary, provides us with no reason not to substitute health values (whether understood as neurosis overcome or as superego escaped) for moral values whenever we reflect on our ultimate ends. And if ethical thought presupposes reflective rationality, as I think it does, not only does this account of idealization leave no place in ethics for substantive ideals, but it also undercuts the rationality of ethical thought even in the sense of resistance to desire on the grounds of allegiance of the will to a principle.

Classical analysis neglects a key element of the rationality of moral values—that role which rational thought must play in order to illuminate reflection *within* the structure of desire. Hartmann uses a broad but fairly standard account of rationality as "logically correct thinking and the consideration of available (outer and inner) data; also the checking on these facts and their connections according to commonly accepted rules" (p. 78). But since, of course, some of this "inner data" is irrational, we are unable to move inside the desire-object tension arc and talk of a rational ordering of ends. "Ultimate ends, then, are considered as psychological givens" (p. 79). Hartmann's lack of a self psychology closes off the ends themselves from introspection. The ends are the ends of a self, but the self cannot know *why* they are his ends, cannot find anything within himself that he owns and which produces those ends self-understandingly. The most the self can know in terms of *why* he has an end is whether it is a consequence of some other, higher-level end that he has.

Not only does this leave what is deepest in desire unillumi-nated by reflection, it also presents a hierarchical image of goals and ideals which I think is psychologically false. Many richly ordered lives do not subsume their ends in a pyramidal hierarchy but have interweaving, intercollating parallel hierarchies of ends, as well as elements which are not hierarchical at all (such as play and dance). To think that the best human life that reason can judge of is one in which the relationships between ends, means, and subsidiary consequence are maximally known and solely acted upon does justice neither to rationality nor to ideals. It asks both too much and too little of us: too much because if ethical reflection must work only in this way we face an arduous intellectual task with the almost certain prospect of failure for an ideal of rational life that is dubious to begin with, and too little because it leaves untapped the resources of the ethical imagination working *within* the structure both of inferential reason and desire. As the self draws the connections, both theoretically and practically, between its abstract ideals and its concrete circumstances (both inner and outer), it gains a self-awareness that is at once ethical and rational—*not* because it has arranged its ends into a theoretical hierarchy and at last knows how to act, but because its ideals have been released into the structure of its concrete motivation.

Incorporating the argument of the last chapter, we may now assert that the difficulties experienced by Freudians in finding a satisfactory place for the self's ideals within the matrix of autonomy, morality, and rationality stem from its original ambiguity over the concepts of ego and *self*.[23] In effect, as Freud's notion of *Ich* diminished in scope from the self in general to the system ego, the corollary notions of ego-idealization and object-idealization had to be similarly circumscribed. This may further be traced to Freud's difficulties in integrating object-relations concepts into a systemic metapsychology. Freud's ego ideal is primarily a systemic concept, positioned theoretically in the framework of intersystemic and intrasystemic drives and defenses. But the ethicality of ideals requires the interaction of the structure of the self with the *content* of the ideal, so a developed self psychology as well as a theory of object relations become essential.

Within the Freudian framework, the ideal self, whether in its representational aspect or its structural aspect, has little part to play in the development of moral maturity. Although the two thinkers are polar opposites on the question of the rationality of moral values, Freud shares with Kant the equation of morality with obedience to principle and the fundamental theoretical opposition between such obedience and pleasure. Any intrusion of pleasure or desire into the domain of the ethical must, in this view, result in the diminishment of the self's autonomy. The "true self" is a non-aggression pact between the ego, the id, and the superego brought about by the inability of any one subsystem to seize control of the psyche, a compromise in the face of inevitable psychic conflict. Stated differently, the true self of classical psychoanalysis is the ego insofar as it has been able to realize effective adaptations to the demands of instinct life, memories, and the world.[24]

CHAPTER 9

Heinz Kohut's Psychoanalytic Self Psychology

In essence then, I believe that man's destructiveness as a psychological phenomenon is secondary; that it arises originally as the result of the failure of the self-object environment to meet the child's need for optimal—not maximal, it should be stressed—empathic response.

Heinz Kohut, *The Restoration of the Self*[1]

THE BIPOLAR SELF

Attempts to derive the self from one or more elements of the id-ego-superego model of the human psychology, whether in representational or in structural terms, seem either to fail to account for the complexities of subjective self-experience or to lack a viable account of psychic agency. The psychoanalytic self psychology of Heinz Kohut[2] offers a new[3] approach in which structural and representational concepts receive a new alignment, and where the tripartite psychic system (particularly in Kohut's later work) becomes only secondary in explanatory importance. Here, the self is treated as a superordinate structure possessed of both dynamic and representational aspects. In its genesis and early stages of development, it is coincident with the whole of the psyche. Later, it begins to act as an integrating system for the functions of the subsystems and eventually becomes capable of autonomous development.

Kohut's early work derives from Hartmann's conception of narcissism as a cathexis, not of the ego, but of the self.[4] In *The Analysis of the Self* (1971), Kohut saw the self forming out of primary narcissism as a compound of nuclear narcissistic structures, the grandiose self and the idealized parental imago. In *The Restoration of the Self* (1977), he began to distinguish a narrow

99

sense of self as a content of the tripartite mental apparatus (p. 207n) and a broader sense of the self as a superordinate structure under which drives and defenses are subsumed. This is a bipolar structure which has, in it maturation, a set of normally self-assertive ambitions as one pole and a set of integrated ideals and values as its other. Between these poles lies a pool of gradually developing talents and skills that are activated by the tension-arc that establishes itself between ambitions and ideals.[5] Life goals may stem from either pole of the self or from the awakening of talents and skills.[6] (A goal is not simply a mental content, but a combination of contents and actions, p. 216).

The bipolar self is superordinate to both drives and representations. It is essentially enmeshed in object relations which, through identification, constitute the self's internalized nuclear ideals. But its structure does not remain static at the point of (a) merger with the parental ideal; there must follow (b) "de-idealization and transmuting internalization of the idealized omnipotent self-object, and (c) integration of the ideals with the other constituents of the self and with the rest of the personality" (p. 217).

In *Restoration of the Self*, Kohut breaks away from the tripartite model of classical analysis, which he calls a "conflict psychology" (p. 78). On the conflict model, the psyche is viewed as a system of forces (drives), counter forces (defenses), and interactions of forces (compromise formations such as the symptoms of the psychoneuroses), all operating within the hypothetical space of the tripartite psychic apparatus (p. 223). This conflict may take many forms: defenses versus drives, ego versus id, drive maturation versus drive regression (or drive fixation), ego development versus ego regression (or developmental arrest). The model looks on man's psychological condition as "characterized in essence by the conflict between his pleasure seeking and destructive tendencies (the drives), on the one hand, and his drive-elaborating and drive-curbing equipment (the functions of the ego and superego), on the other" (p. 132).

For self psychology, on the other hand, "the drive experience is subordinated to the child's experience of the relation between self and the self-objects" (p. 80). In this view, drive fixations and compulsions are a product of undeveloped self-structure due to empathy failures on the part of self-objects: "The unresponded-to self has not been able to transform its archaic grandiosity and its archaic wish to merge with an omnipotent self-object into reliable self-esteem, realistic ambitions, and attainable ideals" (p. 81). A self-object is an object that is experienced as part of the self—e.g., the child's early experience of aspects of his or her parents. Healthy maturation of the self, whether in the natural development of the child or in the transferences of the analytic session, requires a two-step sequence: (1) empathic merger with the self-object's mature psychic organization as a genuine object (i.e., an independent center of initiative) and (2) the performance of need-satisfying actions by the self-object. Drive psychology's failure to acknowledge the importance of the first step has led to a lack of clarity, in terms of health goals, about the criteria for termination of analysis:

> Some of the most persistent resistances encountered in analysis are not interpersonally activated defenses against the danger that some repressed psychological ideation will be made conscious by the analyst's interpretations or reconstructions; they are mobilized in response to the fact that the stage of understanding—the stage of the analyst's empathic echo of or merger with the patient—has been skipped over. (p. 88)

Empathic response to a child's nuclear self is not so much a matter of conscious encouragement and rebuke, but a deeply anchored responsiveness of the self-objects, which, in the last analysis, is a function of the self-objects' own nuclear selves (p. 100). By repeated empathic response (or lack of it) to the child's exhibition of grandiosity (nuclear ambition), emerging talents, and admired images (nuclear ideals), the child's innate potentials are selectively nourished or thwarted. Destructive rage and sexual perversion are not, ultimately, internal failures to tame drives, but failures of the self-object to meet the need for optimal (not maximal) empathic response: "The primary psychological configuration, however short-lived, does not contain destructive rage but unalloyed assertiveness" (p. 119). Failure of empathic merger results in a narcissistic imbalance, resulting in the creation of either defensive or compensatory structures: "After the breakup of the primary psychological unit (assertively demanded empathy-merger with the self-object), the drive appears as a disintegration product; the drive is then enlisted in the attempt to bring about the lost merger (and thus the repair of the self) by pathological means" (p. 128).

The independent self emerges out of a primary self-object matrix involving "two basic psychological functions—healthy self-assertiveness vis-à-vis the mirroring self-object [and] healthy admiration for the idealized self-object" (p. 171). Within this matrix, a two-stage process of development will typically occur. The first stage is the development of a *nuclear self* through processes of selective inclusion and exclusion of structures from the original matrix:

> This structure is the basis for our sense of being an independent center of initiative and perception, integrated with our most central ambitions and ideals and with our experience that our body and mind form a unit in space and a continuum in time. This cohesive and enduring psychic configuration, in connection with a correlated set of talents and skills that it attracts to itself or that develops in response to the demands of the ambitions and ideals of the nuclear self, forms the central sector of the personality. (pp. 177–78)

As ideals and ambitions distinguish themselves out of the original grandiosity and exhibitionism of the self-object matrix, a "tension arc" is established between these two poles constituting the abiding flow of psychological activity which defines the person as he or she is "driven" by his or her ambitions and "led" by his or her ideals.

Overlayered on this nuclear polarity is a second set of processes which account for the specific developmental direction of the self. Here, defects in either the mirroring-approving self-object or the admired-idealized self-object are compensated for by the development of self-constituents in the more functioning dimension of the matrix. Pathology of the self results only when *both* dimensions are crucially inadequate: "Either the idealized self-object failed the child after the mirroring one had failed or the mirroring self-object failed again when the child attempted to return to it for the remedial sustenance after the destruction of a tentatively delimited self by the traumatic failure of the idealized self-object" (p. 190).

METAPSYCHOLOGY

Kohut's differences with the classical tradition begin at the clinical, rather than the theoretical, level. The diversity of clinical data, he argues, require both a narrow and a broad psychology of the self—one in which it is treated as a content of a mental apparatus, and one in which it is treated as the center of a psychological universe. The first belongs to the drive theory of classical psychoanalysis, the second is the province of Kohut's self psychology. The need for this twofold approach, Kohut argues, is that Freudian analysis is based on a too narrowly scientistic base to meet the restorative goals of analysis: "Freud's values were not primarily health values. He believed in the intrinsic desirability of knowing as much as possible" (p. 64). The psychological phenomena that lie within the domain of self psychology, however, require broader notions of objectivity and rationality than that of the nineteenth-century scientist, one which included introspective-empathic observation as well as participation by the self in the process of understanding. This holds true for both psychoanalytic practice and for our own self-understanding.

Empathy, for Kohut, is defined "as the counterpart of the analysand's free associations—i.e., as the emergence and use of the analyst's prelogical modes of perceiving and thinking" (p. 251). Empathy is as essential in the analytic environment as it is in the human environment at large: "Man can no more survive psychologically in a psychological milieu that does not respond empathically to him, than he can survive physically in an atmosphere that contains no oxygen" (p. 253). This contrasts with Freud's famous dictum that analysts should "model themselves during psychoanalytic treatment on the surgeon who puts aside all his feelings, even his human sympathy."[7] Indeed, Kohut argues, much of the 'resistance' to analysis noted by Freudians are simply reactions of the analysand to the analyst's excessively muted empathic response: "a mixture of disappointed lethargy (enfeeblement of the self) and rage (regressive transformations of the self's assertiveness)."[8]

Consistent with his clinical starting points, Kohut is markedly cautious about the theoretical finality of his concept of the self. Understanding of the self is always through generalization derived from the empirical data gained through the analyst's empathic identifications with the patient's sense of self at succeeding levels of analysis. Although psychoanalysis can conceive the structure of the self within the mental apparatus and its position as center of the individual's universe, it can in no way provide a metaphysics of the self. It is worth quoting him at length because of the implications for moral philosophy:

We cannot, by introspection and empathy, penetrate to the self per se; only its introspectively or empathically perceived psychological manifestations are open to us. Demands for an exact definition of the nature of the self disregard the fact that "the self" is not a concept of an abstract science, but a generalization derived from empirical data. Demands for a differentiation of "self" and "self representation" (or, similarly, of "self" and a "sense of self") are, therefore, based on a misunderstanding. We can collect data concerning the way in which the set of introspectively or empathically perceived inner experiences to which we later refer as "I" is gradually established, and we can observe certain characteristic vicissitudes of this experience. We can describe various cohesive forms in which the self appears, can demonstrate the several constituents that make up the self— its two poles (ambitions and ideals) and the area of talents and skills that is interposed between the two poles—and explain their genesis and functions. And we can, finally, distinguish between various self types and can explain their distinguishing features on the basis of the predominance of one or the other of their constituents. We can do all that, but we will still not know the essence of the self as differentiated from its manifestations.[9]

Some psychoanalysts working within the classical tradition (such as Wallerstein and Rangell) have taken Kohut's remarks on this point as an opportunity to credit him as a clinician only, while seeing no reason to alter or re-examine the tripartite system's *theoretical* primacy. But such a vigorous distinction between the clinical and theoretical levels of discourse is difficult to sustain in this context. Kohut clearly maintains his twofold distinction at the theoretical level also, if at a less grand level of theory than that of "essences" and "natures." To be sure, Kohut's theoretical interests are those of a practicing psychoanalyst. Similarly, philosophical attention to the concept, while it may stop short of talk of essences, can probably not afford to be so phlegmatic about the distinction between structural and representational concepts.

On the other hand, even at the psychoanalytic level, the influence of theory on practice is more significant than Kohut here suggests. Leo Rangell, for example, a vigorous opponent of self psychology, sees its attempt to introduce a concept of a superordinate self as having a clinically damaging effect on patient recovery. At the therapeutic level, he claims, it shifts the focus from the analytic to the existential mode: "Treatment is no longer for what the patient suffers but for what he is."[10] This creates a fear in patients that they, rather than their neurosis, will be changed by analysis. Rangell therefore favors the structural school,[11] which does not promise 'restoration' of the self, but, at best, a 'synthesis' (after Nunberg) or 'integration' (after Hartmann). These latter metaphors seek to bring out the belief inherent in classical psychoanalysis that it is conflict, not unity, which is both prescriptively and descriptively the fundamental condition of the self: "Normalcy is an amalgam of contradictions."[12] Wallerstein, while stressing "the wholeness of psychoanalysis within its one (Freudian) paradigm"[13] at the theoretical level, more sympathetically advocates a 'both/and' approach for classical psychoanalysis and self psychology at the clinical level (especially concerning the treatment of narcissism).[14] At the theoretical level, however, Wallerstein remains committed to the conflict model of compromise formation and conflict accommodation which sees psychological ill-health as capable of relief but not cure: "The normal and neurotic are different in degree but not in kind."[15]

Wallerstein rightly notices a tension in self psychology between its broad metapsychological view of the self and its advocacy of a 'complementary' partnership with classical psychoanalysis. But it is a moot point how much of this is due to inner contradiction or to the rhetorical necessity of the times: Kohut was originally a favored son of classical analysis and perhaps sought to ease the shock of his paradigm shift by suggesting a compromise. A similar point may be made about Wallerstein's and Hanly's objection that "the problem with the psychology of the self as a theoretical orientation for therapy is that it disconnects the treatment of narcissistic conflicts from the concurrent and sequential treatment of object libidinal conflicts."[16] It is not obvious that this is any more than a complaint that the theoretical languages don't mesh very well, which is surely to be expected in competing paradigms.

Wallerstein's main point of issue with self psychology, however, is over its rejection of classical analysis' guiding model of the psyche as a conflict of drives and defenses in favor of a model which speaks of experiences of deficit or restoration. Like Rangell, Wallerstein points to a number of recent theoretical innovations more or less *within* the classical tradition which *do* address the more superordinate and intrasystemic dynamics covered by self psychology. The work of Sandler on the unconscious preemptory urge,[17] for example, bridges explanatory lacuna between intrasystemic and intersystemic conflict. In addition, classical analysis has been broadened by the recent emphasis on developmental consideration spurred by child psychology (e.g., the work of Mahler, Pine, and Bergman) so that intrapsychic conflict may be linked with phase-specific biological changes and developmental tasks stemming from innate, environmental, and experiential forces. Dorpat[18] in particular makes a useful distinction between structural conflict (conflict between psychic instances in the developed personality structurally differentiated along tripartite lines) and object-relations conflict, conflict "between the subject's wishes and ideals, injunctions, and prohibitions that are not experienced as his own, but rather as represented in primary- or secondary-process representations of some (usually parental) authority."[19]

Wallerstein, like Rangell, complains of the tendency of self psychologists (particularly those with a more polemical style, such as Ornstein)[20] to caricature classical analysis and ignore recent developments (although a reading of the institutional journals reveals that this is hardly a one-way affair). Undoubtedly much of this heat is due to the present state of psychoanalytic theorizing about the self, a result of the confusion and entrenchment that surrounds an essentially contested concept. Wallerstein is perhaps too sanguine about the ease with which representational and object-relations concepts may be accommodated to the classical tradition. On the other hand, self psychology can hardly claim, at present, to have emancipated itself from the conflict vocabulary of classical analysis. Wallerstein points out that the language of self psychology often includes words such as *tension, anxiety, avoidance, frighten,* and *danger* which, he says with some justice, are part of the vocabulary of the drive model. He also notes that self psychologists sometimes fail to make the distinction between conflict and pathology. Health for Wallerstein is the "mastery of conflict."[21] The Oedipus complex is "the universal psychological nodal point of the human developmental drama."[22] "It is not that 'oedipal strivings' are pathological but that they are conflicted that is vital to their classical understanding and to the evolved psychoanalytic theory of development."[23]

According to Wallerstein, behind self psychology's switch from a conflict to a deficit model there is a move to locate pathology in the psyche's environment rather than in the individual psyche itself. By moving away from the classical Freudian definition of psychoanalysis as dealing with the phenomena of transference and resistance to an empathy-failure model, self psychology locates developmental failure in other people's empathy failure and therapeutic failure as the fault of the analyst: "a not so subtle shifting of the responsibility (and the blame) for therapeutic difficulty unfairly (i.e., one-sidedly) onto the interfering countertransferences of the analyst" (583). The result, according to Treurniet,[24] is that the patient "is deprived of his autonomy as he is deprived of his drives."[25]

The charge that the locus of responsibility has been shifted from analysand to analyst is quite true, but the implications for autonomy are less obvious. Questions of responsibility and autonomy lie at the heart of many of the issues between classical analysis and self psychology. It perhaps seems odd that Freudians attack self psychologists (who, after all, are arguing for a model of human psychology in which genuinely integrated selfhood is a possibility) on the grounds that they deny human autonomy and freedom. But if we remember that the classical model sees agency individualistically and treats both environmental support and lack of support as essentially limiting to the domain of individual 'will,' then such objections become more intelligible. Yet it is doubtful that the rather cumbersome notion of 'will' has a place in contemporary theories of motivation. It is a folk-psychological accompaniment to the ethics of principle. And the implied model of autonomy which is being defended by classical analysts seems to be only the negative freedoms of freedom from external constraint and freedom from (extreme) inner conflict.

There is more to responsibility and autonomy than this. Responsibility is intentionality (reflective purposiveness) and accountability for one's life and actions. A psyche operating under defensive or compensatory structures lacks the reflective capacity for genuine internal accountability (i.e., conscience). It is therefore appropriate that the analyst bear the responsibility for cure: that is the task of psychoanalysis. The same holds true for the wider social context. Healthy selves are internally accountable for the restoration of selves in deficit. The enormity of this project does not invalidate it as a necessary social ideal. And concerns about criminal responsibility of pathological individuals largely miss the point. A self incapable of internal accountability can nevertheless be held accountable to others. This may seem unjust. That "society's to blame" is indeed frequently true, but juridical punishment can only operate on retributive principles in fairness to others (especially victims). At the same time, however, it is morally incumbent on us to create a retributive system (with all due consideration for the rights of prisoners) in which aspects of what may at first be seen as 'punishment' are actually restorative processes. This puts the utilitarian goal of reform in a new light: it is actually not aimed at the good of the whole at all, but performed out of respect for the dignity of the prisoner.

Self psychology, in fact, clarifies the moral meaning of autonomy. What we respect is the intrinsic value of persons—their autonomy. But this autonomy is not, as it is for Kant, their ability to act according to their conception of universal laws. It is their ability to be guided by imaginative ideals (and integrated ambitions) that are truly their own. An individual in psychological deficit does not have fully actualized autonomy, but the developing self is still at work, and it is to this nucleus of personhood that our respect is directed. The meaning of moral concern is likewise interpreted. It is not a choice that we make, but the natural empathic response of self to self, stemming from our own nuclear experience in the family self-object matrix.

Self psychology is presently faced with two ultimately joined research tasks. The first is to provide a theoretical account of the superordinate self as an autonomous agent, structurally connected to the processes previously identified via the postulate of an intrapsychic system of id, ego, and superego but nevertheless capable of autonomous, integrated action distinct from these determinants. The second is to provide an account of how representational concepts contribute to this autonomy. While classical psychoanalysis has developed sophisticated structural concepts, it has tended to ignore (with the significant exceptions of Sandler and Kernberg)[26] representational dimensions of the self. According to Kohut, this has led to its failure to develop certain introspective concepts necessary to effective therapy).[27] Self psychology has a number of provocative suggestions about the unities between structural and representational concepts, but because of its relative newness, it lacks a large body of crucial clinical data and detailed theoretical elaboration. There is at present no clear account of how the two groups of concepts may be united. Drive-structure concepts alone lack the necessary depth of intention for autonomy. Representational concepts may provide this, but cannot then rest within a traditional ontology of psychically isolated selves possessed of a 'power' of will.

It is not my purpose here to provide an alternative ontology of the self, nor to settle all the current debates between classical psychoanalysis and psychoanalytic self psychology. Given the present state of the question, such determinations would be clearly premature. The answer to these questions lies considerably beyond the scope of this book. My purpose in this chapter and the next is merely to outline a psychology of the self sufficient to clarify the place of ideals, considered as schematizing procedures for interpreting concrete situations in terms of their relevance to the realization of what the self takes to be its good life. For this purpose, it seems to me that self psychology provides the most promising line of research. As we shall see in the next chapter, the Freudian attachment to the pathology model rather than the health model—or, in Kohut's terms, an attachment to the model of "Guilty Man" rather than "Tragic Man"—makes an adequate treatment of the positive role of idealization in ethical reflection highly problematic.

It should also be kept in mind that the debate over the self is not merely between classical psychoanalysis and self psychology. Some mention should be made of the approaches to the self by what Ticho[28] has called "the alternate schools of psychoanalysis": the schools of Adler, Jung, Horney and Sullivan. Adler's notion of the creative self, Jung's conception of the self as an archetype expressing the individual's need for unity and wholeness, Horney's conception of a neurotic tension between the ideal self and the real self, and Sullivan's notion of a self dynamism operating within a real world of interpersonal relations (rather than intrapsychic object relations)—all of these have received significant and loyal, if somewhat isolated and factional attention (with Sullivan's ideas perhaps making the most inroads into classical psychoanalysis). The presence of these schools gives the debate a truly kaleidoscopic character, depending on which set of theoretical allegiances one views it from. It remains true, however, that the most sustained (and, to my mind, the most significant) investigation of the self is the self psychology of Heinz Kohut.

CHAPTER 10

Narcissm and Ethical Idealization in Self Psychology

Grandeur progresses in the world in proportion to the deepening of intimacy.

Gaston Bachelard, *The Poetics of Space*[1]

Three points of difference can be observed in psychoanalytic self psychology which distinguish it from classical psychoanalysis on the issue of idealization. First, idealization is not a feature of some subsystem of the psyche, but rather a feature of the superordinate self structure. Second, idealization as it relates to moral values is not primarily a feature of oedipal conflict, but rather a feature of earlier and different psychodynamics—namely, the dynamics of infantile narcissism. And third, idealization need not in any way be pathological, or limited to the realm of fantasy: it is one of the crucial means by which the self restores itself in the face of conflict and trauma.

As we saw in the previous chapter, according to Kohut a nuclear self is formed out of archaic mental contents very early in infancy. In his early work, Kohut described the origin of the self as the consequence of the inevitable disturbance of the infant's blissfully experienced primary narcissism due to experienced defects in parental (usually maternal) care.[2] A nuclear bipolar structure of grandiosity and idealized goal structures is established which receives rapid consolidation between the ages of two and six.[3] Retaining Hartmann's definition of narcissism as libidinal cathexis of the self, Kohut had originally described the maturation of the self in terms of the ego gaining control of these structures so as to develop a healthy object love. The grandiose self becomes incorporated into the ego as ambition, the idealized parental imago is transmuted into the ego ideal.[4] At this point he still viewed the self as a representational subcomponent of the ego. But he had already given the ego considerably more scope than that of "conscious control." In his first book, *The Analysis of the Self*, Kohut described optimal development as a transition from an archaic matrix of mirroring self-objects through a phase of decathexis of narcissistic libido to authentic object love grounded in mutuality. Disruption of this process may lead to narcissistic personality disorders such as phase-inappropriate grandiosity and the clinging to archaic ideal objects.[5]

In his later work, Kohut became less interested in accommodating self-pathology to conflict psychology and advanced a new paradigm of human psychology under the rubric of "Tragic Man." Freud's "Guilty Man" describes a psychology of pleasure-seeking drives stemming from single functions of body and mind which, in conflict with parental responses, produce guilt and anxiety. Tragic man, on the other hand, is seeking self-realization through parental responses toward what can be experienced in a larger, coherent, and enduring organization.[6] Failures of response bring, not guilt and anxiety, but shame and empty depression:

> Guilty Man lives within the pleasure principle; he attempts to satisfy his pleasure seeking drives, to lessen the tensions that arise in his erogenous zones. . . . Tragic man, on the other hand, seeks to express the pattern of his nuclear self; his endeavors lie beyond the pleasure principle.[7]

The former model, Kohut argues, is appropriate only to the more limited sphere of structural conflict neuroses. Unconscious infantile layers of the ego are striving to protect the personality from the fears experienced in the conflict of drive-wishes and perceived threats (e.g., castration anxiety). The latter model is required to understand the more fundamental narcissistic personality disorders:

> Classical theory cannot illuminate the essence of fractured, enfeebled, discontinuous human existence: it cannot explain the essence of the schizophrenic's fragmentation, the struggle of the patient who suffers from a narcissistic personality disorder to reassemble himself, the despair—the guiltless despair, I stress—of those who in late middle age discover that the basic patterns of their self as laid down in their nuclear ambitions and ideals have not been realized. Dynamic structural metapsychology does not do justice to these problems of man, cannot encompass the problems of Tragic Man.[8]

In *Restoration of the Self*, Kohut proposes a new model of human psychology. The concept of the bipolar self as a superordinate structure becomes central. In the case of Tragic Man, resistances to psychic health are due to disintergration anxiety on the part of the archaic nuclear self which does not want to re-expose itself to the narcissistic injury produced by failure to have its mirroring and idealizing needs met. The result is that the self fails to be solidly established independently of its self-object transferences. It requires the presence of the self-object rather than transforming it into a psychological structure which can operate independently through self-generated patterns of initiative (ambitions) and inner guidance (ideals).

One of the reasons why a new metapsychology is required, says Kohut, is because human psychology is presently undergoing significant change. Whereas in the past psychopathology stemmed principally from "emotional overcloseness" (p. 269) in a close family unit, today the family unit is threateningly distant:

> Where children were formerly *over*stimulated by the emotional (including the erotic) life of their parents, they are now often *under*stimulated; where formerly the child's eroticism aimed at pleasure gain and led to internal conflict because of parental prohibitions and the rivalries of the oedipal constellation, many children now seek the effect of erotic stimulation in order to relieve loneliness, in order to fulfill an emotional void. . . . It is clear that children often undertake both solitary sexual activities and group activities of a sexual, near-sexual, or sexualized nature in the attempt to relieve the lethargy and depression resulting from the unavailability of a mirroring and of an idealizable self-object. (pp. 271–72)

Human psychopathology has begun to shift its center from the arena of guilt-ridden overstimulation and conflict to that of inner emptiness, isolation, and unfulfillment. Today:

> It is the understimulated child, the insufficiently responded-to child, the daughter deprived of an idealizable mother, the son deprived of an idealizable father, that has now become paradigmatic for man's central problem in our Western world. (p. 286)

The primacy of the self concept in Kohut's work required a reevaluation of the narcissistic matrix in which it was formed. As Chessick has pointed out, in classical analysis narcissism is viewed as a term with negative value, at least from a developmental perspective.[9] The canonical psychiatric manual, DSM-III,[10] broadly describes the narcissistic personality as one who combines a sense of self-importance with an exhibitionistic need for attention and admiration. It is accompanied by unrealistic feelings of entitlement, a lack of empathy for others, and a propensity toward interpersonal exploitation.

Self psychology suggests that this overly emphasizes the disorder aspects of narcissism. Phase-appropriate narcissism may be part of the restorative process at all levels of maturity. Chessick,[11] for example, shows how a writer may recover narcissistic equilibrium after public rejection through attention to the details of his craft, leading to an enlarged vision of the world, a sense of humor, and an invigorated self. Kligerman[12] has offered a detailed analysis of how, after narcissistic wounding, an artist may strive to regain original nucleic wholeness by reconstructing the ideal self or self-object as a concrete work of art. In pathology this may take on an "almost addictive need to create," as in the life and grandiose suicide of Yukio Mishima. But it would be a mistake to interpret the link between the passionate integrity of great art and deeply felt deficits in the self in all cases to pathology. Exhibitionism and crucial idealization are beneficial components of the process of creativity. The analysis of narcissism can be usefully extended to illuminate a host of human situations. Strozier[13] describes the idealizations and narcissistic transferences in the leader-follower relation (Freud and Fliess, Gandhi and Nehru, Hitler and Speer). Mason[14] and Greenlee[15] have studied the idealization-exhibitionism process as it leads to integration of the self in religious life.

Kohut's theory of narcissism has two dimensions: that concerning the grandiosity of the self, and that resulting in the idealized parental imago (whereas object love has a separate line of development). Grandiose self (especially) and idealized parental imago are phase-appropriate self-object transferences, which make possible belated maturation of the self. Under optimal conditions, ideals and ambitions are developed as primary structures of the self. Traumatic dysfunctions could cause defensive structures to develop. Finally, later mirroring or idealization could restore the self's continuity by producing compensatory structures.[16] Transference in analysis requires therapeutic regression to the point at which normal development of the self was interrupted, and permits the reactivation of healthy growth processes. This is how analysis cures.

Contrary to classical analysis, Kohut did not view narcissism as a defense against the Oedipus complex. In clinical observation, instead of a reactivated Oedipus complex in the form of a classical transference neurosis, Kohut found that " ... despite some simultaneous anxiety, the brief oedipal phase [at the end of an analysis] is accompanied by a warm glow of joy—a joy that has all the earmarks of an emotionality that accompanies a maturational or a developmental achievement."[17] This led him to emphasize the essentially healthy and adaptive aspects of the oedipal period. Whereas classical analysis treated it as the nucleus of neurosis, self psychology treats it as a matrix in which the self establishes independence and autonomy.

Kohut's new approach to the oedipal period prepares the ground, I believe, for a revised moral psychology. Classical psychoanalysis has traditionally equated moral psychology with the analysis of the superego which, in turn, has been called by Freud "the heir of the Oedipus complex." In the conflict model, the Oedipal complex is described in terms of an ego motivated by castration anxiety, retreating to the chronic adoption of defensively held narcissistic positions. According to Freud:

> Religion, morality, and a social sense—the chief element of what is highest in man—were originally one and the same thing. According to the hypothesis which I have put forward in *Totem and Taboo* they were acquired phylogenetically out of the father complex: religion and moral restraint by the actual process of mastering the Oedipus complex, and social feeling from the necessity for overcoming the rivalry that then remained between the members of the younger generation.[18]

In self psychology, the conflicts of the Oedipal period presuppose a firm and active superordinate self.[19] They may occur at any stage of life, and may indicate a healthy struggle for self-consolidation in the face of disintegration anxiety:

> Any person afflicted with serious threats to the continuity, the consolidation, the firmness of the self will experience the Oedipus complex, despite its anxieties and conflicts, as a joyously accepted reality. (p. 229)

Although classical psychoanalysis may adequately cover most of the pathological elements of this period, its presuppositions prevent it from seeing the positive elements within the framework of a broader health model (rather than simply a successfully lived-through oedipal phase). For Kohut, while the risk of castration anxiety, narcissistic injury, and competitive aggression are very real, a more profound joy is also arising as the child transforms its self-object matrix into genuine selfhood. We can see that an intimate space of parental love has been transferred without loss into an inward intimacy. The joy springs from the intimation of new experiences, as well as the pride and joy emanating from the parental self-objects "despite—indeed, also because of—their recognition of the content of their child's oedipal desires" (p. 236). What classical analysis had treated as a universal human experience is in fact a pathological variant of a broader oedipal state which is potentially both exhilarating and pleasurable.

Kohut's model of the self, I believe, provides a way of viewing ethical life which is *neither* simply a function of social or cultural context (as espoused by relativism) *nor* a Kantian bondage of the desiring self to psychically external universal principles. Kant grounds his distinction between humans as moral agents as opposed to beings who are determined by the laws of 'nature' (a word which we must take to mean the universe *sans* selves) on the distinction between reason and inclination. There is a fundamental difference, he claims, between actions for the sake of principle and actions for the sake of pleasure. In a similar vein is Freud's distinction between the id's pleasure principle and the compulsive externality of the superego's moral demands. But in self psychology, the link between pleasure, rationality, and concern for others remains intact through the progress of developmentally continuous ideals.

Classical psychoanalysts correctly points out that both ego idealization and idealization of others involve the early incorporation of the "pleasure ego."[20] But this by no means excludes it as a source of moral motivation. If ethical rationality is loosened from its concern with universal principles to focus on the origin of valuation in idealization, moral motivation can be seen to be both rational and intrinsic to the self. This is possible only if the concept of idealization is not restricted to the infantile desire to internalize powerful objects, or to revel in images of self gratification, or to delude oneself with fantasies of being a perfect self, or to excoriate oneself for failing to be that perfect self. A psychology of ethical idealization requires us to understand idealization as a natural 'inner' dynamic, not the measurement of self against not-self.

Idealization has usually been thought of in essentially representational terms: a person imaginatively represents to himself an ideal object (whether self or other), and then by various strategies (whether of the ego or the id) seeks to obliterate the distance between the actual self and the ideal object. The pathologies of perfectionism and irrational guilt arise as a frequent natural consequence. In classically interpreted narcissism, this stems from the desire for invulnerability and the desire to maintain nuclear gratification. It aims at an identity whose self-enjoyment is immune from the vicissitudes of concrete life. But a more constructive view of idealization sees it in structural terms. Idealization is not fundamentally the representation (or image) but the schematizing structure which produces it. To be sure, this is frequently accompanied by representations of what we deem our ideal and actual self, but healthy obliteration of the distance between these representations and our perceived actual self is not a matter of repressing or falsifying one or the other representation. It is a structural project that reinterprets ourselves and our relations with others so as to bring our life into line with our self understanding.

Structurally, the self is not so much guided by the accuracy of its self-representations as it is by its urge toward integration. Idealization, along with appropriate ambition, is the primary strategy by which a fragmented self regains cohesiveness.[21] That the self originally possesses this cohesiveness is a tenet of Kohut's psychology of the child. The nuclear self is "psychologically complete so long as it breathes the psychological oxygen provided by contact with empathically responsive self objects. . . . "[22] Restoration is possible to the degree that "at least one sector of the personality has been established in which an unbroken continuum (from one pole of the self to the other, i.e., [1] from ambitions, via [2] skills and talents, to [3] ideals) of functioning self structure enables the individual to carry out the basic program of his specific nuclear self."[23]

Whereas Kohut's notion of idealization as a primary structure of the nuclear self places the etiology of its development before the psychological structures that develop as a consequence of internalization, Freud viewed all forms of idealization which were not narcissistic as a consequence of object internalization. Only this last form of idealization was connected to morality (namely in the workings of the superego). Such a psychology drove moral theory to two stark and depressing conclusions, which continue to haunt many people. First, it led to a view of morality as imposed on the self from without. Little room is available for concepts of moral autonomy and maturity. Second, with the internalization of objects came the internalization of the compulsive threat that the object bore which led the self to internalize it in the first place.[24] The result is that questions of right became inextricably bound up with questions of justifications for compulsion. Right could *only be* might. But compulsion is not a reflexive notion—one cannot compel oneself to act—so a divided self is inevitable.

The distinction between compulsion (coercive power over another) and authority failed to be clearly drawn in Freudian moral psychology. Authority is the legitimation for the exercise of power. But that legitimation may proceed either by establishing the right to compulsion (law) or by embodying an ideal. It is my argument that personal ideals *can* exercise authority over us to the degree that they recognizably originate in the most authentic part of our self to which we have access. The authority that our ideals possess is something like the Socratic notion of individual conscience: ethical autonomy is adherence to one's ownmost or best 'voice' (although the metaphor has now been changed to that of seeing-as, and we can now give some account of its positive content). One *sees* ethically. One's best knowing is released into the structure of one's motivation through the schematism. A deficit, in Kohut's terms, is made good.

This remains true *even though* ideals are not generalizable in the way that principles are (although they may be shared by a large number of people). Some of these ideals are recognizably ethical in that they originate in a respect for persons insofar as they are persons. Others are more closely tied to the self-understanding of one's autonomy and manifest themselves as ideals of responsibility. Still others emanate from the more archaic matrix of the nuclear self and express themselves as deeply felt ideals of concern. These ideals, when given substance by the developing understanding of the self, carry with them all the motivating power of feeling and inclination. To exclude these motivational resources, as Kant does from the domain of morals proper, is to strip morality of its psychodynamic connection with the concrete subject.

The result is an impoverishment of our concepts of both morality and rationality. Personal ideals are relegated to the domain of inclination, and rationality becomes severed from the concrete. Kant called inclination "the deceiver within ourselves,"[25] and his rejection of feeling as a guide to what is right or as a component of value is notorious: "Those who cannot think expect help from feeling."[26] The point to be made here is not, of course, that if an act 'feels' right then it is right, but that morally educated seeing-as can sometimes provide a surer guide (perhaps, at times, the *only* guide) than a set of inferences from principle. And a good part of what is meant here by moral education is integration of the self with a reflectively developed set of ethical ideals.

In addition, a theory of ideals rehabilitates the role in ethical life of the unconscious, considered broadly as that which is concretely active in us but about which we are unaware. It is not simply an irrational psychic structure, a burden to be overcome by a principled consciousness and a pure will. It is the nuclear source of our idealizations and the constant companion of our ethical reflections. Freud rightly saw that it is the unconscious which is behind the experience of conscience; but we are now able to interpret that in a constructive manner—not as alien internalization interfering with the autonomy of the ego, but as a representative within the structure of our motivations of the needs of the restoring self.

At the same time, moral reflection is rescued from the charge of rationalization. Kohut's analysis points to the role in healthy consciousness of self-understanding considered as a concrete reflection prior to, and necessary for, competent abstract knowing.[27] If we see mental health as the movement from disintegration anxiety to self-cohesion rather than from castration anxiety to conflict resolution, conceptual contents need not be made to take the responsibility for personal well-being.[28] It is not a matter of an essentially conflicted psyche achieving accommodation with its environment by acting according to what it knows conceptually to be the best course even though its "inclinations" may tend otherwise (the Kantian "will enslaving desire" model). In the self-psychological model, the cohesive center of personality deals more directly with its environment in terms of ambitions and ideals operating at motivationally deeper levels within the psyche than that of conceptual content.

With the growing self-awareness of maturity, these restorative impulses are knit together with a gradually elaborated set of ideals formed in our concrete relations with others. Ethicality enters with this self-awareness, not as an external compulsion on the self (one cannot simply will one's ideals to be ethical), but as an expression of the ongoing synthesis of ideals and concrete relations with others.

In this way, the ethically good remains a part of the natural history of consciousness. The self's good is to be understood naturalistically as that which satisfies desire. But desire can be seen to operate within restorative, defensive, or compensatory structures of the self. The framework of the classical drive machinery perhaps adequately accounted for defensive structures and somewhat less adequately accounted for compensatory structures, but it did not at all account for the operation of desire in the primary moral structures of the self. Kohut's self psychology permits us to locate the ethically good within a moral psychology which does not require an interpretive rupture between description and prescription, between is and ought.

PART 3

Conclusions and Implications

CHAPTER 11

Moral Authority for a Free People

> This spiritual Love acts not nor can exist
> Without Imagination, which, in truth,
> Is but another name for absolute power
> And clearest insight, amplitude of mind,
> And Reason in her most exulted mood.
> William Wordsworth, *Prelude*[1]

AUTONOMY AND AUTHORITY

The aim of this book has been to develop a theory of ideals suitable for incorporation into a concept of ethical life and action. The concept of idealization, as it has been developed here, is that of a psychological structure with both outward and inward dimensions. Outwardly or objectively, it is a seeing-as: a schematic procedure for interpreting objects by attending to some aspects and not others. Which aspects are attended to will depend on the structure of the attending subject. Inwardly or reflexively, idealization is a psychodynamic operation within the structure of the subject. In classical psychoanalysis, this inward idealization is treated either as a fantasy mechanism in which the self seeks to evade the demands of reality or as a division within the psyche between the self and the not-self (i.e., the self I ought to be but am not—the superego). In psychoanalytic self psychology, this inward idealization is treated as both a process internal to the self and one which, instead of being placed in opposition to reality, is a crucial means by which the self accommodates itself to, and integrates itself with, that reality. I have argued that it the latter notion is a more useful framework for a moral psychology of ideals.

Kant rightly saw that an adequate account of the ethical must explain the basis for two essential marks of ethicality: autonomy and authority. Kant's insistence on this point, one of his greatest achievements as a moral philosopher, raised the level of discussion

beyond that of the eighteenth-century sympathy theorists who
sought to replace ethical theory by a natural history of morals.
Kant explicated both these concepts in terms of rationality, and
rationality in terms of the universality of principles. The *motivation* to act rationally springs from an element of the person which
Kant called "will," as opposed to "inclination." Only the will
could be autonomous, and only human beings (so far as we
know) have will. The will he defines as "a faculty of determining
itself to action in accordance with the conception of certain
laws."[2] His definition of autonomy is equally clear:

> Autonomy of the will is that property of it by which it is a law
> to itself independently of any property of objects of volition.
> Hence the principle of autonomy is: never choose except in such
> a way that the maxims of the choice are comprehended in the
> same volition as a universal law.[3]

Autonomy gives Kant his positive conception of freedom. He
defines freedom negatively as independence from foreign causality. From a theoretical point of view, negative freedom is not
available to human beings, as this would place us altogether outside of connection with the system of causality which is nature:
"What else, then, can the freedom of the will be but autonomy,
i.e., the property of the will to be a law to itself."[4]

The authority of moral principles, for Kant, follows from our
twofold awareness of laws as applying universally, and ourselves
as rational beings (i.e., beings who can act according to their conception of laws). Kant asks: "But why should I subject myself as a
rational being, and thereby all other beings endowed with reason,
to this law?"[5] His answer is that the self (i.e., the reflective awareness) of the rational being is subjectively necessitated to it insofar
as it thinks of itself as free: we "assume a different standpoint
when we think of ourselves as causes a priori efficient through
freedom from that which we occupy when we conceive of ourselves in the light of our actions as effects which we see before our
eyes."[6] Ethical authority, then, in its manifestation to the subject,
derives for Kant from a form of self-consciousness in which our
theoretical understanding of ourselves as implicated in the net-
work of causality is in some sense abrogated.

This "different standpoint" of self-consciousness, for Kant,
points us toward our true self, a true self that cannot be experienced in concrete reflection: "A man may not presume to know

even himself as he really is by knowing himself through inner sensation."[7] Nevertheless, because he is a rational being who cannot think of the causality of his own will except under the idea of freedom, he does have a form of consciousness of his own true inner activity:

> But beyond the characteristic of his own subject which is compounded of these mere appearances, he necessarily assumes something else as its basis, namely his ego [*Ich*] as it is in itself. . . . [I]n respect to that which may be pure activity in himself (i.e., in respect to that which reaches consciousness directly and not by affecting the senses) he must reckon himself as belonging to the intellectual world.[8]

This moral world is not the world of theoretical understanding, but the world of autonomous action on the authority of principles—i.e., the world of "pure practical reason." Other approaches to autonomy, however, are possible. Autonomy—literally "self-law"—is a pregnant word in moral discourse, and it has been endowed with many shades of meaning in the history of thought.[9] These variations are evoked by the differences in such explications of autonomy as 'self-determination,' 'self-government,' 'self-direction,' 'self-mastery,' and 'self invention.' In its broadest sense, perhaps, autonomy may be defined as the condition of being motivated by goals and priorities which are truly one's own. This is the one adopted in the theory of ideals.

Authority, also, has been variously described. Watt[10] traces its origin to the Latin *auctoritas*, related to *auctor*. Lewis and Short's Latin dictionary defines *auctor* as: "He that brings about the existence of any object, or promotes the increase or prosperity of it, whether he first originates it, or by his efforts gives greater permanence or continuance to it." In my own view, authority is the legitimation for the exercise of power. As such, it falls completely neither into a typology of power nor a typology of right, but rather partakes of both. One can have power without authority and authority without (external) power. Authority may be seen as power exercised rightly or right operating in the domain of power. By power, I mean the ability to act—to do something intentionally. This ability, in turn, stems from one's ability to marshall forces, focused units of energy, within a particular domain of operation.

Kant takes the legitimation for the exercise of power as a question of establishing the right to compulsion. Compulsion presupposes externality. So if moral rules are to be imperative for us, they must possess their authority externally to our concrete self (namely, in their universality for all rational beings). But, armed with an adequate psychology of the self, we can surely identify a meaningful sense of authority which is internal to the concrete self—the authority which comes from embodying an ideal. This is authority in the sense of leadership (as distinct from command). Our ideals do not compel us, but lead us.

The question that a theory of ethical ideals seeks to answer is "How are both autonomy and authority possible at the level of personal ideals?" For it would seem that if ideals are "merely" those large aims that one chooses oneself in a concrete way, they lack the authority to command us which Kant saw as one of the key mark of the ethical. The answer offered here is twofold. Formally and objectively, the authority stems from the fact that the ideal is characterized by valuations of respect, responsibility, and concern for persons insofar as they are persons. But this generates no substantive maxims, and the ethicality of ideals cannot be judged by whether or not they pass a test of universalizability. The formal criterion simply rules out some ideals as unethical or nonethical.

A positive determination requires an examination of the concrete motivational dynamics of the self. Ideals are ethical to the degree that the schemata of interpretation which prompt us to respond to our world in a manner characterized by respect, responsibility, and concern are perceived by conscience to be restorative of the continuity and integrity of the concrete self. This perception is at the same time our means of self-understanding, our dynamic of moral life, and the authoritative warrant for our ideals. Such a conscience is not intuitive in any mysterious or mystical way. It is a concrete process of reflection in which reason is not abandoned, but rather transformed into an illuminative imagination. It may take considerable time, or it may be almost instantaneous if the restorative work has already been accomplished. And to say that such a conscience is the ultimate authority for adult human beings is not to say that its determinations at any particular time have absolute validity. After all, the degree to which our motivations are transparent to our reflection may vary considerably. Some people have more developed consciences than others. The point is that, regardless of our degree of self-understanding, we have no other moral authority than our own conscience: even when we turn to others for guidance, that guidance must be filtered through our self-understanding.

The account I propose differs from Kant's conception of ethics as denoting a domain in which a subjectively good will submits itself to a course of objectively right actions as determined by a principle of maxims. In my view, principles are secondary, and the primary determinant of the ethical domain is the motivational-interpretive structure of the self. Further, I wish to extend the scope of the ethical beyond right actions to include right attitudes, right understanding, and right self-images. Not only do these historically predate actions, but the world of the self is far more dense than what directly manifests in action. One advantage of such a conception of ethics is that it establishes notions of ethical autonomy and authority without appeal to transcendental categories or selves belonging to an intellectual world, positing no self beyond the concretely living and acting self 'willing' the actions of the concrete self. Another advantage (although there will be some inclined to see it as a disadvantage) is that it allows room for the individual to refuse to submit to a principle, and yet remain within the sphere of the ethical (e.g., disobeying the principle 'Don't lie' when the Nazi asks where your sister is hiding). It ties the notion of right to what the concrete self takes to be good. The good is not an intellectual being or form. It exists in time to the extent that a person's life is shaped by his experiments with truth in the domain of the right.

Ideals are rich in contents tracing their origin through a course of developments which begin in the narcissistic enjoyments of the nuclear self. They are schematizing structures for interpreting circumstances in terms of what the self take to be its good life. The notion of good here precedes a categorization by appeal to principles. It is the self's good—i.e., whatever the self deems good. When, in healthy moral development, the self begins to perceive its good in terms of relations of respect, responsibility, and concern with others, what has happened is *not* an abandonment of narcissistic enjoyment, but a certain self-clarification of the enjoying self. To be sure, it is one's own unique self that is one's special care, but it is at the same time a self which shares the same or similar structure with all other selves. This recognition permits a transfer of one's dynamic of self-relation to other persons, without any sense that one is sacrificing oneself in the process. Indeed, there is a gain in that one's own self-relations become clarified and purified: one is much more sure what it is about oneself that is *worth* one's attention.

This gives us a clue as to what constitutes sympathy in its genuinely ethical sense. Not all feeling with others is ethical: taking pleasure in the pleasure of another is clearly not ethical sympathy if that other's pleasure derives from malice or egoism. The moral psychology of sympathy has yet to be described in contemporary psychoanalytic language, although Kohut's empathic merger seems to provide a good starting point. Just as, within the self, narrow self-interest can be distinguished from proper self-love on the basis of the degree and manner in which idealization processes are involved, so genuine sympathy for others will be mediated by a concern for those processes in the other.

What distinguishes ethical ideals from other ideals in a structural way is whether or not they originate in respect, responsibility, and concern for the dignity, welfare, and happiness of persons. Their substantive content is filled in by the culture, personal history, and path of self-development of the individuals concerned. Together, these can generate general, but not universal, principles. Killing, lying, suicide, and theft may *all*, under some rare circumstances, be the right thing to do. They remain wrong in an ideal sense, however, and that means a real sense. When we act contrary to our ideals, as we sometimes must, our path of growth, integration, and restoration is hindered. We therefore have the responsibility, as well as (in the non-defensive and non-compensatory personality) the desire, to work toward altering the conditions that made that choice necessary.

Concretely (i.e., in terms of the self's actual motivations), the good is what the self takes to be good in the way of actions and relations which move it in the direction of its restorative ideals. In the largely unselfconscious life of the child, such ideals are little more than empathic merger-mirror responses in the child's selfobject matrix. In adult life, these ideals receive much more representational structure, which then mediate the self's imaginative schemata in a manner requiring much more self-reflection. While Kant may have been right to give some primacy to respect in mature reflective moral consciousness, for it to have motivational force it must be connected to more archaic sources in the self. Respect itself *does* have a rational structure, both in terms of the inner psychology of the subject and in terms of the schematic apprehension of objects. But respect is a component only of rationality *in concreto*; it is not a counter of abstract thought. Abstract universalizability has nothing essentially to do with it.[11]

It is not part of my thesis that health values and ethical values are necessarily coextensive. Although I believe they generally intersect, it is possible that some restorative ideals are opposed to ethical ideals. This might especially be true when these later ideals are established in compensatory rather than primary self-structures.[12] But the subjective grounding of the restorative ideals in the empathic matrix would at least make this an unusual result. Whether or not they do in fact coincide is in any case an empirical question. And whether the one can conceptually be reduced to the other probably cannot be shown at the theoretical level. Theory and therapy, after all, perform different functions. To demand more than this would seem to be an extreme standard to which an ethical theory should be held accountable. One wants to say with Aristotle that theory can only be precise as its subject matter permits.

But I believe that a moral psychology based on self psychology does significantly recast the ways in which the relation between health values and ethical values can be understood. Whereas for classical analysis health values were individual while moral values were social in origin, we can now relocate a significant portion of ethical authority within the concrete individual self. In particular, the relation of respect involves the honoring of the autonomy of the other (in Kant's terms, treating others never merely as means, but as "ends in themselves"). Such a relation seems only psychologically possible to the degree that the self has literally internalized the autonomy of the other. Just as for Freud internalization of parental figures was in reality the internalization of the superego of the parents, so in our view the "transmuting internalizations" of self psychology are actually the internalizations of the ideals of parental figures. Because what is internalized includes autonomy, however, this involves no loss of self but rather defines the original conditions from which restorative ideals may develop.

VIRTUE ETHICS RECONSIDERED

What are the connections between ethics, happiness, and mental health? Virtue ethics in the classical form it received from Aristotle posits a very close connection. All human beings strive to be happy; happiness (or well-being) consists in the possession of certain excellences or virtues (*arete*) of character; and mental health consists of a combination of theoretical wisdom about the world (*sophia*) and practical wisdom about how it is best to live (*phronesis*). The good self is the happy self is the sane self. Today, of course, we are aware that many people who are not good are quite content with themselves; many people who *are* good seem to be quite miserable much of the time; and many people with low self-esteem seem particularly adept at understanding the world in realistic terms.[13] In addition, we are deeply committed to the belief that there are many ways of pursuing happiness, and the idea that there are common criteria of happiness for all seems to be both empirically false and politically dangerous. But a number of our misgivings about any solid connection between the three can be removed by a careful consideration of what Aristotle was and was not saying.

Virtue, for Aristotle, is a mean between two forms of vice in our actions and passions, one of deficiency and one of excess. Virtues are moral absolutes in two senses. First, for any situation, a virtuous person is capable of discovering the optimally right thing to do: "There are many ways to be in error . . . but there is only one way to be correct."[14] Second, certain kinds of feelings and actions are absolutely wrong and admit of no mean: "The names of some automatically include baseness, e.g., spite, shamelessness, envy, and adultery, theft, murder."[15] At the same time, however, the mean is relative to the person and situation involved, and in many cases it is subject to degree. What might be the optimally right action for one person may well not be so for another person in a different situation. It is perfectly consistent with Aristotle that an act which might require great courage of one person might be regarded by another in a similar situation as not a courageous choice at all. In addition, abstract formulae of right have little relation to the concrete situation and must be left to the best judgment of the person involved: "As a condition for having a virtue, the knowing counts for nothing, or for only a little."[16] So, amid an essentially healthy absolutism, Aristotle has a great deal of healthy relativism as well.

It might be thought that this relativism does not go far enough, that Aristotle is too sanguine about the specific content of the virtues. This objection has some bite. We are all aware that there is some degree of cultural shift in the determination of moral character. Adultery, for example is not equally condemned around the world. Alasdair MacIntyre has done good work in rehabilitating the content of the virtues, however, by relativizing them to social practices without thereby eliminating their meaning as excellences of personal character:

> The virtues therefore are to be understood as those dispositions which will not only sustain practices and enable us to achieve the goods internal to practices, but which will also sustain us in the relevant kind of quest for the good, by enabling us to overcome the harms, dangers, temptations and distractions which we encounter, and which will furnish us with increasing self-knowledge and increasing knowledge of the good.[17]

This is a modification, I believe, that Aristotle would accept. It is fully within the spirit of Aristotle's philosophy, while at the same time it accommodates modern sensitivity to variant cultural context. It does mean, however, that we will need a leaner notion of what counts as morally absolute as well as a more elaborated psychology of the emplacement of the virtues in the self if we are to make any firm connection between ethics and mental health. In my view, the moral virtues are ingrained idealizations. The three absolutes for the self in moral space that I have put forward in this book are respect, responsibility, and concern. To be sure, these can be given somewhat different content in different situations and cultures. And to be sure, even in similar cultures and situations, different persons can legitimately spread moral contents and meanings in different patterns along this superordinate matrix—some people being more morally activated by respect for dignity, some by sympathetic concern for suffering, and some by a sense of personal responsibility. Nevertheless, if the connection I have argued for between these and Kohut's genealogy of the self in terms of growth, integration, and restoration is correct, then there is a real and necessary relationship between moral life and mental health. In that sense they are absolute. The absoluteness is claimed on empirical and theoretical grounds. It is not a priori. Were selves to manifest their developmental paths radically differently from the way that the data of experience and clinical analysis indicate, then the claim would have to be revised. Similarly, were human selves to evolve in the future to points where these three values were not relevant to psychological development, we should also have to revise our theoretical claims. But we can safely leave that discussion to the moment of encounter with those beings, rather than assume that the mere possibility of it refutes the understanding that these values are absolutely central to human psychological health. On a more realistic note, cultural differences over moral valuations can only be settled after they have seriously and extensively investigated and engaged with each other. To declare a priori with the relativist that they *must* by definition have equally profound moral achievements is as philosophically and psychologically naive as is the cultural imperialist's belief that his or her culture *must* be the superior one in all significant aspects.

Regarding the argument over the connection between ethical life and happiness, we can again get some important preliminary resolution from Aristotle. The aim *(telos)* of human life, for Aristotle, is happiness. Happiness *(eudaimonia)* is the activity of the psyche in accordance with virtue or excellence *(arete)*. The Greek word *eudaimonia* is only loosely translated as happiness, the English word carries connotations that the Greek word does not have, and vice versa. It literally means well-spiritedness, or well-being of the psyche in its activity. For Aristotle, then, happiness is not something that we achieve or are given, but rather something that we perform. At least this is true for happiness in its most complete meaning. Aristotle's common sense leads him to acknowledge a secondary need for certain external goods as well: "We cannot, or cannot easily, do fine actions if we lack the resources.. Further . . . we do not altogether have the character of happiness if we look utterly repulsive or are ill-born, solitary, or childless."[18]

In addition, Aristotle qualitatively distinguishes between happiness and pleasure, whereas in English we frequently tend to conflate them (at most distinguishing happiness as longer-term and more profound pleasure). For Aristotle, happiness is a psychological activity, pleasure is a psychological condition (an "affect" we might say today). It is quite consistent with Aristotle, therefore, that someone striving to do the right thing could at the same time be feeling miserable, as could a ruthless criminal take pleasure in his ill-gotten gains and in the suffering of his victims.

However, having qualitatively distinguished them, he reconnects them in moral life: "Virtue of character is concerned with pleasures and pains."[19] People make the choices they do ultimately because they believe they will feel pleasure or avoid pain.

In Kohut's terms, we are motivated by our primary narcissism. When we do something which we *know* to be right but which causes us psychological pain, Aristotle would say that we are not in full possession of a virtue: "If someone who abstains from bodily pleasures enjoys the abstinence itself, then he is temperate, but if he is grieved by it, then he is intemperate."[20] In Kohut's terms, the locus of pleasure and pain has shifted from primary self-structure to compensatory or defensive structures. The 'natural' life of good persons for Aristotle is full of pleasure: "Their life does not need pleasure to be added [to virtuous activity] as some sort of ornament; rather, it has its pleasure within itself."[21] In Kohut's terms, they experience joy in the growth, integration, and restoration of their authentic selves. That this happiness or joy often seems to escape us goes without saying. But people who have carried some of it over into their adult life unerringly recognize it on their moral horizon, are motivated by it as part of their ideal, and are prepared to move toward it in ambition despite considerable secondary pains along the way.

A more serious difficulty for virtue ethics concerns what I have called the 'natural' life of good persons. Why is it necessary that our happiness be pursued in accordance with virtue? Aristotle's answer, of course, is drawn from his physics. Everything in nature, including human beings, has a natural end toward which it is striving, a *telos*, which determines its process of development and proper function (*ergon*). This function, in turn, is determined by the specific difference that marks off one species from another, designating its form and essence. The specific difference of human beings is their capacity to reason. So their peculiar function is to think and act with reason. Reason establishes the virtues by discovering the mean between extremes. The moral virtues are simply reason at work in actions and passions, one's way of performing the function of one's species. Since all humans share the capacity to reason, the virtues are the same for everyone, even if their style and degree of manifestation may vary.

Despite its neat elegance, this argument faces several objections. First (and most obviously), even a casual observation of human life reveals that we pursue a plurality of goods that do not seem readily subsumable under the single good of happiness. But two arguments by Aristotle mitigate much of the force of this. First, the many goods that we seek are either good as a means to some further good or good in themselves. In the latter case (e.g., conversation, listening to music, adventure, etc.), Aristotle claims that analysis reveals that whatever good these possess *just is* the activity of reason in passion and action. Second, a natural end is different from a psychological purpose so that, however much we believe that some activity makes us happy (e.g., taking drugs, pulling legs off flies), we will be mistaken if it is not in conformity with virtue. This may not fully convince us, but it does mean that virtue ethics is not refuted by casual observation of the plurality of human ends.

A second objection directly challenges the notion of teleology (or natural finality) upon which classical virtue ethics depends. It is simply not true that the things of nature have an in-built design which establishes their essence and proper function. Not only is the doctrine of fixed form refuted by Darwin's theory of evolution, but the physics upon which it depends—the four causes, the hierarchy of beings, characterless matter, entelechies, and the movement from potentiality to actuality—has been outdated ever since the rise of seventeenth-century science. This is not the place to enter into a discussion of what might be saved of Aristotelian physics in the light of contemporary scientific theory. The objection is a powerful one. Contemporary Aristotelians have tended to grant the force of the objection for the world of facts but argue that it does not apply to the world of human values. Because of their capacity to reason, human beings (unlike other beings) *are* teleological creatures. They are capable of acting on the basis of ends conceived by reason as necessary to their self-realization.

The third difficulty, of course, as I hope this book has shown, is that our values are ultimately products of imagination rather than reason. This would not be fatal, however, if an intelligible psychological account could be given of how imagination might be integrated with reason. Unfortunately, Aristotle's psychology rules out the possibility of imagination as a foundation of rational moral understanding. In *De Anima III, 3-8*, Aristotle distinguishes sensation from the human faculty of thinking, with imagination (*phantasia*) as the bridge. He hesitates between assimilating imagination to sensation or to reason. Eventually he opts for the former, and describes imagination proper as a movement in the soul, resulting from sense perception, and producing an image stored in memory which thinking then uses as a content for its operation: "The soul never thinks without an image."[22] He adds that there is also a metaphorical meaning of imagination in which we might describe it as part of the process by which we judge and deliberate concerning that which is true or false. It is the literal, image-making sense of the term, however, which came to dominate his psychology of thinking. This had profound effects on the development of Western philosophy, entrenching the empiricist attachment to mental imagery and helping to seal imagination's fate as a capacity irrelevant to truth.[23] It also rendered the imagination useless as an avenue through which autonomous beings might apprehend the good: "Someone might say that all men strive for the apparent good, yet no one is in control of the imagination; rather how the end appears to someone depends on what sort of man he is."[24]

Aristotle, I believe, made the wrong theoretical choice here. He should have taken the metaphorical use of the imagination as primary. It is precisely the seeing-as capacity outlined in Chapter 4, only we now see that it is not merely a metaphor for deliberation but a genuine cognitive ability in its own right. It *is* to some degree within our control—namely, when the mature self-structure adapts the imagos of the good that it inherits from its original self-object matrix to both its understanding of reality and to the identity needs of its developing life. What sort of man or woman one is depends as much upon how the end appears to one as the other way around.

This revision frees virtue ethics to speak of the natural life of self-realization *without* having to rely on a concept of human nature as possessed of a fixed essence determining its good—beyond the structural conditions of respect, responsibility, and concern. It also untangles some obscurities in Aristotle's concept of *phronesis* (practical moral wisdom). Aristotle asserted, but never clearly explained, that reason operates to discover the mean in the "non-rational" part of the soul (desire and appetite). It is not rational, but nevertheless it "listens to reason." How? Aristotle is driven back to rely on the external compulsions of habituative training: "By chastening, and by every sort of reproof and exhortation."[25] We can now see that desire listens to reason because imagination is at the same time both desire and reason, indeed reason in her most exalted mood. And of course this carries with it a much more voluntaristic and psychologically sensitive approach to moral education.

THEORY AND PRACTICE: RELATIVISM AND
THE THEORETICIAN'S DILEMMA RECONSIDERED

Concrete ethical reflection originates in a realm of consciousness lying between the abstractions of principle and the pre-reflective identifications and repulsions of the unconscious. It is a domain where the concrete content of many principles originates and also where ethical choices are made not to follow a principle in a particular case. This is the domain of imagination. But it is also open to reason, not in the sense that it proceeds according to the laws of inference, but in the sense that the imagination may operate here within the space of reasons—shaping that space by its very operation. Imagination's work, in the form of mature ethical idealization, is neither opposed to reflection on principle and attention to consequences, nor is it simply an heuristic process operating independently of them. It is an integral part of a concretely unified ethical rationality.

It is true that a theory of ideals places certain limits on the degree to which ethical questions may be settled in the abstract. Philosophy cannot claim to understand that which lacks a representation. And the self, at least in part, is always other than its representation. But both the clinical evidence adduced by psychoanalytic self psychologists and the theoretical necessity of rendering key moral concepts intelligible require the centrality of the concept of the self in understanding our moral life. That part of the postmodern project, then, which has focused on a "decentering of the self," is misguided.[26]

Moral philosophy, then, has not reached a dead end, but arrived at a point where it can make new alliances with other human explorations, notably psychology and psychoanalysis. The clear perception that abstract reason fails to resolve the nodal difficulties of relativism and the theoretician's dilemma has occasioned much grieving among dedicated philosophers. But (in the language of psychoanalysis) this temporary object loss can be overcome if we integrate the enormous best of past philosophy into a restored self of reason. We can acknowledge the truth of Newman's remark in *Apologia Pro Vita Sua*: "It is the concrete being that reasons; pass a number of years, and I find myself in a new place; how? the whole man moves; paper logic is but the record of it." Such a statement is not in opposition to reason, but perfectly balances that champion of articulate thought, René Descartes:

Like one who walks alone and in the twilight, I resolved to go
so slowly, and to use so much circumspection in all things, that
if my advance was but very small, at least I guarded myself from
falling. . . . I observed in respect to Logic that the syllogisms and
the greater part of the other teachings served better in explaining to others those things that one knows (or like the art of
Lully, in enabling one to speak without judgment of those things
of which one is ignorant) than in learning what is new.[27]

Imagination is also a vehicle of understanding, mediating
between the abstract prescriptions of principle and the concrete
requirements of circumstance and desire. This does not so much
commit us to psychologism as to lead us to re-evaluate the
obscure relation between ethical theory and ethical practice. This
is especially necessary in ethics, the general theory of right practice in personal relations. The quotation from Aristotle at the
beginning of this book should be our guide.

Right relation between ethical theory and ethical practice pro-
hibits us from treating the two as fundamentally separate activities. But it also enjoins us against determining our theoretical
choices according to the degree to which they forward certain
social causes to which we are attached. Ideology ought to have as
little place as possible in the momentum of inquiry. Moral intelligence is now at a point where it can afford neither an inconse-
quential preoccupation with the minutiae of ethical theory nor an
irrational ideology of practical commitment. The twin poles of
theory and practice must draw from the same well of reflective
imagination in such a way that they are mutually transformed.

Both the problem of relativism and the theoretician's dilemma
lose much of their force once a distinction in rationality is admit-
ted between abstract theory construction and concrete reflection.
The authority problem in relativism is resolved once we see that
moral authority arises in the ideals of the concrete self. For adults,
the wisdom of others, even when real and substantial, has no
authority over the self until the necessary work of internalization
has been done. Similarly, our own desires and ambitions possess
no moral authority either, until they have been integrated with
our ethical ideals. The problem of discernment in relativism (how
can we judge between alternative accounts of the right if they
spring from different concrete visions of the good?) is resolved by
concentrating on the development and maintenance of our own
ideals while giving them as much exposure to alternatives as pos-

sible. Discernment will take care of itself as the self internalizes what it needs. The theoretician's dilemma disappears once one realizes that moral wisdom is a matter of schematizing one's field rather than (a) getting a true theory of universal right, (b) working out how to apply that theory in practice, and (c) overcoming the motivation problem known as weakness of the will.

Much of the battle between absolutists and relativists can be seen, then, to be based on a misunderstanding. The hard part in ethics is not whether morals are 'absolute' or 'relative.' For *of course* ethics, like everything, is relative. It is relative to the ways in which we must choose to live, it is relative to what we understand, and it is relative to reality. And *of course* ethics, like everything, is absolute: if something *really is* right for us to do, then it is absolutely right for us to do it. Because reality is what it is, it is absolutely what it is. The more deeply our ideals and principles are sourced in our self-understanding, the more absolute they become. The more absolute they become, the more substance is required to be furnished by relative imaginations. Both in discerning the rightness or wrongness of visions of the good markedly different from our own, and in knowing the right in particular cases, an earnest reason may rightly seek the aid of an ethical imagination. In this way theory is seen to enter practice neither as an enemy of concrete desire nor as an agent of self-deception bearing emblems not its own, but concretely and on it own terms—at once as friend, guide, and restored offspring.

DEMOCRACY AND MORAL AUTHORITY

A political philosophy emerges from this which cuts across the usual distinctions between liberal and conservative thought. A good society does indeed place high premium on individual determinations of the right and good and strives to maximize the environment for personal autonomy. But this is not because it lacks a rational means of discriminating the worse from the better, nor because it thinks the apparatus of government should take only minimal responsibility for the moral condition of society, but because it realizes that healthy group norms are the product of the developed ethical imagination of individuals. The practical implications for social policy are that (1) significant resources should be directed to cultivating ethical imagination and understanding,

(2) such cultivation should be a condition for individuals' holding positions of responsibility, and (3) considerable autonomy should be granted to persons in such positions. At present, the reverse policy of each of these three proposals is usually pursued. But a democracy will not survive without morally educated citizens entrusted with responsibilities commensurate with the full expression of their personhood.

The development of our public life calls for a deeper appreciation of the lasting harmonies between wisdom and democracy. The need to go beyond nonjudgmental pluralism does not have to force us into claiming knowledge of moral truths placed in a transcendental realm. Rather, we need commitment to the *context* of wisdom. Not all wisdom is to be found in the context of theoretical philosophy—indeed, there are certain important kinds of wisdom that of necessity must be found elsewhere—but a great deal more can be found there than those who, out of fear of the totalitarian implications of Platonism, support a democratic leveling of ideas would imagine.

If universities (and moral teachers generally) have a legitimate ideology, it is this commitment to the context of wisdom. This ideology, in its effects if not in its inspiration, will be undemocratic. It will declare that not all ideas and ideals are equal, that some are deeper, broader, and more insightful than others, and that this difference can be shown to exist to anyone who is willing to be guided by critical and reflective thought. At the political level it will reveal itself as a commitment to increase the number of forums in which reason rather than power-interest rules, to judge our potential leaders according to their wisdom first and their ideology second, and to fight for ways to increase the chances that our candidates are not merely survivors in the pragmatics of electioneering, but people able to turn a keen reflective eye to the large questions of what is good and right in human affairs.

At the same time, moral education is education for democracy. The goals are the same: life which is both autonomous and good. The fact that much of our life together is neither of these cannot entitle us to coerce beyond the point that justice and the true autonomy of those coerced is thereby served. This coercion will go beyond the principle of only coercing when the safety of others is in question (for that is simply an abandonment of our responsibility to the morally damaged), but it will stop well short of any pseudo-Platonic philosopher despot. When we understand the necessities of the self's path to restoration, intrusion on autonomy is as painful as it is wrong.

Human beings are at the same time both individuals and members of communities. Nevertheless, the two require somewhat different analytic treatment. Individuals cannot simply 'read off' their ethical standards from the principles, practices, and ideals (real or espoused) of their society. It will be readily agreed that, from a practical point of view, this is neither possible nor desirable. But, more than this, public moral debate and private ethical reflection require, in part, different modes of understanding. Central to private ethical reflection is the use of imagination, but the imagination is a capacity of individuals; it is only in a derivative and artificial sense attributable to groups. Group norms, *qua* norms, are not designed to deal with uncodified experience. The individual, on the other hand, faces situations every moment which invite an infinite depth of reflection beyond the coded level. He or she must, of necessity, be an imaginative artist.

Does this imaginative artistry prevent the reflection from being genuinely rational or genuinely ethical? I think not. While we all would acknowledge the importance of both art and thought, we have perhaps become too comfortable with Kierkegaard's distinction between the artist and the ethical thinker as different *types*. A civilized society, to be sure, requires the division of labor. The thinker and the artist perform different functions with different motives and with different canons of legitimation and models of excellence. At the cultural level of norms and practices, this separation has undoubtedly been beneficial to both: the introduction of the standards of the one into the activity of the other has almost always resulted in aridity in art or romanticism in thought. But an individual, finally, is not a crowd. The tasks of art and intellect must, at some point in a life, be performed by the same person at the same time to the same end.

NOTES

PREFACE

1. Aristotle, *Nichomachean Ethics*, trans. Terrence Irwin (Indianapolis: Hackett, 1985). II. 2, 1103b, 27.

CHAPTER 1. CONTEMPORARY DILEMMAS IN THE PROJECT OF ETHICAL UNDERSTANDING

1. Samuel Johnson, *The Rambler*, vol. 2, ed. W. J. Bate and Albrecht B. Strauss (New Haven: Yale University Press, 1969), 300. no. 125, 28 May 1751.
2. Plato, *Euthyphro: The Dialogues of Plato*, vol. 1, trans. B. Jowett (New York: Random House, 1920), 388–93.
3. For an intellectual history of modern casuistry, see Edmund Leites (ed.), *Conscience and Casuistry in Early Modern Europe* (Cambridge: Cambridge University Press, 1988).
4. This unconvincingness has been admirably illuminated by Philippa Foot in "Morality and Art," *Proceedings of the British Academy 56* (1970): 131–44.
5. This is a problem similar to what Gadamer in *Truth and Method* (New York: Crossroads, 1982) has called "the problem of application" (274f). But there is a difference in scope: the problems facing the theoretician at the juncture of theory and practice are not only problems of application; they are also problems of discernment, self-understanding, etc. For a recent discussion, see John Howie, ed., *Ethical Principles and Practice* (Carbondale, Il.:Southern Illinois University Press, 1987).
6. A special issue of *The Monist* has recently been devoted to this problem (vol. 67, no. 3: 1984). See also Alasdair MacIntyre, *After Virtue*, 2d ed. (Notre Dame Ind: University of Notre Dame Press, 1984); Stuart Hampshire, *Morality and Conflict* (Oxford: Blackwell, 1983); and Gilbert Harman, "Moral Relativism Defended," *Philosophical Review 34* (1975): 3–22.
7. T. K. Seung, *Semiotics and Thematics in Hermeneutics* (New York: Columbia University Press, 1982), 16.
8. Carl G. Hempel, "The Theoretician's Dilemma: A Study in the

Logic of Theory Construction," *Minnesota Studies in the Philosophy of Science*, vol. 2 (1958), 37–98.

9. *Ibid.*, 49–50.

10. Casuistry had for long been connected with the history of the Jesuit order. In its early manifestations it was just as principle-based as ethics proper, but with the rise of the notion of conscience, casuistry came to be seen as a more practical enterprise. See H. D. Kittsteiner, "Kant and Casuistry," *Conscience and Casuistry in Early Modern Europe*, Edmund Leites, ed. (Cambridge: Cambridge University Press, 1988).

11. For a good intellectual history of the concept of *phronesis*, see Nicholas Lobkowicz, *Theory and Practice: History of a Concept from Aristotle to Marx* (Lanham, Md.: University of Notre Dame Press, 1967).

12. *Nich.Eth.* bk. 6, ch. 4: 1140b6.

13. Gadamer has recently developed this approach within the context of a reappraisal of the tradition of hermeneutics. See Hans-Georg Gadamer, *Truth and Method* (New York: Crossroads, 1982), esp. 274–325. While I think he is right to insist that *phronesis* is a matter of understanding rather than a craft-skill granted simply through the repetitions of experience, I believe that he has overestimated the degree to which problems of ethical practice can be resolved by recourse to the *praxis* of the traditional moral community, and underestimated the element of personal discovery in which moral ideas are presented in a new way to an individual: "But practical philosophy insists on the guiding function of *phronesis*, which does not propose any new ethics, but rather clarifies and concretizes given normative contents" (Hans-Georg Gadamer, letter to Richard Bernstein in appendix to Richard J. Bernstein, *Beyond Objectivism and Relativism: Science, Hermeneutics, and Praxis* [Philadelphia: University of Penn. Press, 1983], 263).

14. Two excellent complementary intellectual histories of the concept are provided by Murray Wright Bundy in *The Theory of Imagination in Classical and Medieval Thought* (Chicago: University of Illinois Press, 1927); and James Engell, *The Creative Imagination: Enlightenment to Romanticism* (Cambridge: Harvard University Press, 1981).

15. Thomas Winter Leddy, "Imagination, Metaphor and Cognition: Inside the Concept," *Dissertation Abstracts International* 43 (1983): 3937A. Boston University

16. Plato, *Phaedrus* (248 a–b), trans. B. Jowett, in B. Jowett, *The Dialogues of Plato*, 2 vols. (New York: Random House, 1937). See also Murray Wright Bundy, *The Theory of Imagination in Classical and Mediaeval Thought* (Chicago: University of Illinois Press, 1927), ch 2.

17. P. F. Strawson, "Social Morality and the Individual Ideal," *Philosophy* 4 (1961): 1–17.

18. Stuart Hampshire, *Morality and Conflict* (Oxford: Blackwell, 1983), 2.

19. *Ibid.*, 165.

20. Stuart Hampshire, "Commitment and Imagination," in *The Morality of Scholarship*, Northrop Frye, Stuart Hampshire, Connor Cruise O'Brien (Ithaca: Cornell University Press, 1967), 44.

21. It is not that these oppositions are not legitimate and important. They are. My point is that they cannot be used to drive a wedge between imagination and reason.

22. This point has been well argued, from different standpoints, by Martin Price, Martha Nussbaum, and William Walsh.

23. I take the ethical neutrality of aesthetic creation to be a central theme of modernist poetics. Martha Nussbaum has recently argued that, at least in the case of the novel, such neutrality is indefensible; that some moral questions are of such concrete complexity that they can only be addressed by a text of equal concrete complexity, i.e. a novel rather than an abstract philosophical work; and, moreover, this moral concern enhances rather than diminishes the aesthetic value of the work. Nussbaum's argument raises key questions about the relations between philosophy and literature, as well as the aesthetic place of the novel. My arguments apply only to those views which hold aesthetic creation to be morally neutral. See Martha Craven Nussbaum, "'Finely Aware and Richly Responsible': Literature and the Moral Imagination," *Literature and the Question of Philosophy*, ed. Anthony Cascardi (Baltimore: Johns Hopkins University Press, 1987).

CHAPTER 2. HUME AND SMITH: IMAGINATION IN THE EXTENSION OF SYMPATHY

1. *Works* 1965. VII, 118.

2. For a discussion of this issue, see Jonathan Dancy, "The Role of Imaginary Cases in Ethics," *Pacific Philosophical Quarterly* 66 (1985).

3. For useful treatments of Hume and Smith see Philip Mercer, *Sympathy and Ethics* (Oxford: Clarendon Press, 1972); W. C. Gore, *The Imagination in Spinoza and Hume* (University of Chicago Press, 1902); and Thomas Douglas Campbell, *Adam Smith's Science of Morals* (London: Allen and Unwin, 1971); R. M. Hare, *Moral Thinking: Its Levels, Method, and Point* (Oxford: Clarendon Press, 1981), chs. 5 and 6, provides an interesting contemporary approach. Alfred Mackay, "Extended Sympathy and Interpersonal Utility Comparisons," *Journal of Philosophy* (June 1986) offers a good critical discussion of some current problems.

4. David Hume, *A Treatise of Human Nature, 1739*, ed. L. A. Selby-Bigge (Oxford: Clarendon Press, 1968), 574–75.

5. *Ibid.*, 589.

6. *Ibid.*, 575–76.

7. *Ibid.*, 584.

8. Hume, *Treatise*, 427.

9. Adam Smith, *Theory of Moral Sentiments*, 2d ed., 1761 (London: Henry G. Bohn, 1853), 3–4.

10. Hume, *Treatise*, 424.

11. Adam Smith, *Theory of the Moral Sentiments*, 323.

12. Such as may be drawn, for example from N. J. H Dent's account of rationally ordered passions in *The Moral Psychology of the Virtues* (Cambridge: Cambridge University Press, 1984).

13. James Engell, *The Creative Imagination: Enlightenment to Romanticism* (Cambridge: Harvard University Press, 1981), ch. 10.

14. See Hume, *Treatise*, 582, and Smith, *Theory of Moral Sentiments*, part 1, sect. 2, ch. 2.

15. It might be objected that, as an ideal sympathizer the impartial (i.e., disinterested but not uncaring) spectator does not require rational legitimation but gains a motive for choice only through an interest in others' interests. David Gauthier has argued that such a model could not support a principle of justice and presents no coherent representation of the ideal sympathizer's self. David Gautier, *Morals by Agreement* (Oxford: Clarendon Press, 1986), 237–38.

16. R. M. Hare, in *Moral Thinking* (Oxford: Clarendon Press, 1981) has recently made a serious attempt to do just this.

17. Max Scheler, *The Nature of Sympathy* (London: Routledge & Kegan Paul, 1954), 12–36.

18. Immanuel Kant, *The Doctrine of Virtue* (part 2 of *The Metaphysics of Morals*), trans. Mary J. Gregor (Philadelphia: University of Penn. Press, 1964), 125.

CHAPTER 3. KANT

1. Immanuel Kant, *Anthropology from a Pragmatic Point of View*, trans. Mary J. Gregor (The Hague: Martinus Nijhoff, 1974), 39, 55.

2. See Engell, *Creative Imagination*, 128–39; Herbert James Paton, *Kant's Metaphysic of Experience: A Commentary on the First Half of the Critique of Pure Reason* (London: G. Allen & Unwin, 1970); Mark Johnson, *The Body in the Mind* (Chicago: University of Chicago Press, 1987), 147–66; and Norman Kemp Smith, *A Commentary to Kant's "Critique of Pure Reason"*, 2d ed. (1923), 260–68, 337–38.

3. Immanuel Kant, *Critique of Pure Reason*, A120.

4. Immanuel Kant, *Anthropology from a Pragmatic Point of View*, trans. Mary J. Gregor (The Hague: Martinus Nijhoff, 1974), 44.

5. James Engell, *The Creative Imagination* (Cambridge: Harvard University Press, 1981. 128–39, esp. 132.

6. I am indebted for this ordering to Mark Johnson's *The Body in the Mind: The Bodily Basis of Meaning, Imagination, and Reason* (Chicago: University of Chicago Press, 1987), 147–66.

7. Kant, *Critique of Pure Reason,* A77, B103.

8. Kant seems also to talk the threefold process as a whole as the activity of the reproductive imagination. See A120.

9. Kant, *Critique of Pure Reason,* A138, B177.

10. Immanuel Kant, *Critique of Judgement,* trans. J. H. Bernard (New York: Haffner Press, 1951), sect. 17.

11. David White, "On Bridging the Gulf Between Nature and Morality in the *Critique of Judgment,*" *Journal of Aesthetics and Art Criticism* 38 (1979), 181.

12. Kant, *Critique of Judgement,* 246. Quoted in Mary Warnock, *Imagination* (Berkeley: University of Calif. Press, 1976), 57.

13. Warnock, *Ibid.,* 58.

14. Kant, *Critique of Judgement,* sect. 59, 198.

15. James K. Mish'alani, "On Moral Imagination," *Man and World* 13 (1980), 197.

16. Kant, *Critique of Judgement,* 197.

17. M. Woods, "Kant's Transcendental Schematism," *Dialectica* 37 (1983), 210.

18. Kant, *Critique of Pure Reason,* A140/B179–A141/B181.

19. For an example of contemporary work by cognitive psychologists in this area, see Allan Pavio, *Mental Representations: A Dual Coding Approach* (Oxford: Clarendon Press, 1986).

20. Charles Larmore, "Moral Judgement," *Review of Metaphysics* (Dec. 1981), 284–85.

21. Kant, *Anthropology From a Pragmatic Point of View,* 71.

22. *Ibid.,* 69.

23. *Ibid.,* 69.

24. Kant, *Doctrine of Virtue,* 73–74.

25. Kant, *Critique of Practical Reason,* 139–40.

26. Kant does admit a third source of motivation, practical reason in its empirical function, which gives us, for example, the promptings of prudence. But he denies that this can serve as a motive to obey the practical moral law: "All practical principles which presuppose an object (material) of the faculty of desire as the determining ground of the will are without exception empirical and can furnish no practical laws" (Immanuel Kant, *Critique of Pure Practical Reason,* trans. Lewis White Beck [Indianapolis: Bobbs-Merrill, 1956], 19). It is true that considerations of prudence can enter into moral judgement in the broad sense, but only negatively, as in setting limitations to temptation. The authority of

the counsels of empirical practical reason is "only as a counterpoise to the lure of vice, to offset in advance the error of rigged scales in practical judgment and so, in the beginning, that the weight of pure practical reason's *a priori* grounds will tip the scales" (Immanuel Kant, *The Doctrine of Virtue* [part 2 of *The Metaphysics of Morals*], trans. Mary J. Gregor [Philadelphia: University of Penn. Press, 1964], 13–14).

27. Kant, *Critique of Practical Reason*, 17.

28. "All material practical principles are, as such, of one and the same kind and belong under the general principle of self-love or one's own happiness" (*Ibid.*, 20).

29. "If a rational being can think of its maxims as universal laws, he can do so only by considering them as principles which contain the determining grounds of the will because of their form and not because of their matter" (*Ibid.*, 26).

30. *Ibid.*, 155.

31. *Ibid*, 163–64.

32. *Ibid*, 164–65.

33. *Ibid.*, 166.

34. Immanuel Kant, *Foundations of the Metaphysics of Morals*, trans. Lewis White Beck (Indianapolis: Bobbs-Merrill, 1959), 17.

35. *Ibid.*, 17n.

36. Kant, *Critique of Practical Reason*, 166.

CHAPTER 4.
THE SEEING-AS CONCEPT OF IMAGINATION

1. Locke, John. *An Essay Concerning Human Understanding* (1690), vol. 2, (London: J. M. Dent & Sons, 1961), 166–67.

2. David Miall, *Metaphor and Transormation: The Problem of Creative Thought*. University of Illinois Center for the Study of Reading, report no. 300. Supt. of docs. no. ED1.310 / 2:237958 (Cambridge: Bolt, Beranek and Newman, 1983); Stephen Michael Kosslyn, *Image and Mind (Cambridge: Harvard University Press, 1980); Anees A. Sheikh, ed.,* Imagery: Current Theory, Research and Application (New York: John Wiley & Sons, 1983).

3. Roger Scruton, *Art and Imagination: A Study in the Philosophy of Mind* (London: Routledge & Kegan Paul, 1974); Gaston Bachelard, *The Poetics of Space* (New York: Orion Press, 1964); Irving Babbitt, *On Being Creative and other Essays* (Boston: Houghton Mifflin, 1932).

4. Dennis Dutton and Michael Krausz, eds., *The Concept of Creativity in Science and Art* (The Hague: Martinus Nijhoff, 1981).

5. R. G. Collingwood, *Principles of Art* (Oxford: Clarendon Press, 1938); Martin Price, *Forms of Life: Character and Moral Imagination in*

the Novel (New Haven: Yale University Press, 1983); William Walsh, *The Use of Imagination: Educational Thought and the Literary Mind* (New York: Barnes and Noble, 1960); Thomas McFarland, *Originality and Imagination* (Baltimore: Johns Hopkins Press, 1985).

6. See James K. Mish'alani, "On Moral Imagination." *Man and World* 13 (1980): 193–206; Mark Johnson, "Imagination in Moral Judgement," *Philosophy and Phenomenological Research* (Dec. 1985): 265–80; Gordon H. Bell, "Imagination and Moral Education," *Journal of Moral Education* 8, no. 2 (1978): 99–109; Philip J. Rossi, "Moral Interest and Moral Imagination in Kant," *Modern Schoolman* 57 (1980): 149–58; G. Reddiford, "Moral Imagining and Children," *Journal of Moral Education* 10 (2): 75–85; P. F. Strawson, "Social Morality and Individual Ideal," *Philosophy* (Jan. 1961): 1–17. Some of these share a traditional Kantian paradigm, others are seeking to break new ground. Much of the newer work gains inspiration from the work of Paul Ricoeur, although prima facie his work seems only tangentially about imagination and not at all about ethics.

7. Edward S. Casey, *Imagining: a Phenomenological Study* (Bloomington: Ind. University Press, 1976), 40–48; Gilbert Ryle, *The Concept of Mind* (New York: Barnes and Noble Books, 1949), ch. 8.

8. René Descartes, *Discourse on Method and the Meditations,* trans. F. E. Sutcliffe (Middlesex, England: Penguin Books, 1977).

9. Ludwig Wittgenstein, *Philosophical Investigations*, trans. G. E. M. Anscombe (Oxford: Basil Blackwell, 1968).

10. René Descartes, "Fourth Meditation," *Discourse on Method and the Meditations*, trans. F. E. Sutcliffe (Middlesex, England: Penguin Books, 1977), 137.

11. Jean-Paul Sartre, *The Psychology of the Imagination*, 2d paperback ed. (New York: Citadel Press, 1963), trans. from the French *L'Imagination, Psychologie Phenomenologique de l'Imagination* (Paris: Galimaud, 1940), 177–78.

12. Hide Ishiguro, "Imagination," *British Analytical Philosophy*, ed. Bernard Williams and Alan Montefiore (London: Routledge & Kegan Paul, 1966), 175–78.

13. Gilbert Ryle, *The Concept of Mind* (New York: Barnes and Noble Books, 1949), 257–58.

14. Ludwig Wittgenstein, *Philosophical Investigations*, trans. G. E. M. Anscombe (Oxford: Basil Blackwell, 1968), 214.

15. Allan Paivio, *Mental Representations: a Dual Coding Approach* (New York: Oxford University Press, 1986).

16. See especially the work of Paul Ricoeur: *The Rule of Metaphor*, trans. Robert Czerny (Toronto: University of Toronto Press, 1977) (translation of *La Métaphore Vive*, 1975); "The Hermeneutical Function of Distanciation," *Philosophy Today* 17 (1973): 129–41; *Hermeneutics*

and the Human Sciences: Essays on Language, Action and Interpretation, ed., trans., and introduced by John B. Thompson (Cambridge: Cambridge University Press, 1981); "Sartre and Ryle on the Imagination," *The Philosophy of Jean-Paul Sartre*, ed. Paul Arthur Schilpp, 1st ed. (La Salle, Ill: Open Court, 1981), 167–78; "The Function of Fiction in Shaping Reality," *Man and World* 12 (1979): 193–206. See also Mary Schaldenbrand, "Metaphoric Imagination: Kinship Through Conflict," *Studies in the Philosophy of Paul Ricoeur*, ed. Charles E. Reagan (Athens, Oh.: Ohio University Press, 1979); Mark L. Johnson and Glenn W. Erickson, "Toward a New Theory of Metaphor," *Southern Journal of Philosophy* 18 (1980): 289–99; W. J. T. Mitchell, "What Is an Image?" *New Literary History* (Spring 1984): 503–37.

17. Cf. Kant, *Critique of Pure Reason*, A141–2, B180–1, who treats the schematism as the means of connecting concepts with images. See also Mark Johnson, *The Body in The Mind* (Chicago: University of Chicago Press, 1987), 156.

18. See Alvin I. Goldman, *Philosophical Applications of Cognitive Science* (Boulder: Westview Press, 1993), 128–30. Mark Johnson has independently developed this idea within the framework of a theory of metaphor. See *Moral Imagination: Implications of Cognitive Science for Ethics* (Chicago: University of Chicago Press, 1993), ch.4 and 189–96.

19. Kant, *Critique of Judgement*, trans. J. H. Bernard (New York: Haffner Press, 1951), 189.

20. Mark Johnson has recently argued that the separation of aesthetic and moral understanding which Kant relies upon is an inheritance of medieval faculty psychology. See Mark Johnson, *Moral Imagination: Implication of Cognitive Science for Ethics* (Chicago: University of Chicago Press, 1993), 207–10.

21. Aristotle, *Poetics* 1459 a 3–8, *Basic Works*, ed. Richard McKeon (New York: Random House, 1941), 1479.

22. Ludwig Wittgenstein, *Philosophical Investigations*, trans. G. E. M. Anscombe (Oxford: Basil Blackwell, 1968), 207.

23. T. E. Wilkerson, "Seeing-As," *Mind* 82 (1973): 491.

24. E. H. Gombrich, *Art and Illusion: a Study in the Psychology of Pictorial Representation* (Princeton, N.J.: Princeton University Press, 1969), 370ff.

25. *Ibid.*, 394–95.

26. Ishiguro (1966), 171.

27. Jean-Paul Sartre, *The Psychology of Imagination*, 7–8. But Sartre is not always consistent on this point, and some of his insights may be treated as useful additions to, rather than objections against, a theory of mental imagery. On this see Lilly Marlene Russow, "A Theory of Imagination," *Dissertation Abstracts International* 37 (1976): 2949A, 31–35.

28. Ishiguro (1966), 176.

29. The notion of imagery covers not only visualizations, but all forms of "sensual" imagery (visual, olfactory, auditory, gustatory, tactile, sensory-motor) as well as verbal imagery (poetic images, word-pictures, etc.)

30. Kant, *Critique of Pure Reason*, trans. Norman Kemp Smith (London: MacMillan, 1970), A141/B181.

31. See Dan Edward Lloyd, "Picturing," *Dissertation Abstracts International* 44 (1983): 192A (Columbia University) for a discussion of causal, intentional, mimetic, and conventional theories, as well as his own theory of the pictorial function.

32. Ludwig Wittgenstein, *Philosophical Investigations*, trans. G. E. M. Anscombe (Oxford: Basil Blackwell, 1968), 213.

33. For a development of the notion of schema as an intermediate functional entity in cognitive processes mediating between the neuronal level and the levels of culture and language, see Michael A. Arbib and Mary B. Hesse, *The Construction of Reality* (Cambridge: Cambridge University Press, 1986). See also Robert W. Howard, *Concepts and Schemata: An Introduction* (London: Cassell, 1987).

34. Paul Ricoeur, *The Rule of Metaphor*, trans. Robert Czerny (translation of *La Métaphore Vive*,1975) (Toronto: University of Toronto Press, 1977), 144.

CHAPTER 5. ETHICAL IDEALS

1. James, William. "What Makes a Life Significant," *Talks to Teachers on Psychology and to Students on Some of Life's Ideals* (1899) (Cambridge: Harvard University Press, 1983), 162.

2. For general treatments of the concept of ideals, see Edgar Sheffield Brightman, *A Philosophy of Ideals* (New York: Henry Holt, 1928); Abraham Edel, *Method in Ethical Theory* (Indianapolis: Bobbs-Merrill, 1963), esp. ch. 15, "The Theory of Ideals"; William James, "What Makes a Life Significant," *Talks to Teachers on Psychology* (Cambridge: Harvard University Press, 1983). More specialized treatments are Joseph DeMarco, "The Role of Ideals: a Model for Applied Ethics," *Philosophy in Context* 13 (1983): 45–51; James N. Loughran, "The Moral Ideal of the Person," *International Philosophical Quarterly* 26 (1986): 147–59; John W. Hennessy and Bernard Gert, "Moral Rules and Moral Ideals: a Useful Distinction in Business and Professional Practice," *Journal of Business Ethics* 4 (1985): 105–16.

3. Richard Wollheim points out that moral psychology has two complementary branches: "On the one hand, moral psychology can be viewed as the study of those mental processes which are involved in

moral deliberation, moral decision, and moral action. It studies moral reasoning, its nature and the defects to which it is susceptible. It is a synchronic study. On the other hand, moral psychology can be viewed as the study of the growth of the moral sentiments, moral beliefs, and moral habits in the typical life-history of the individual. It studies the moral sense as this develops from birth to death. It is a diachronic study. . . . " (Richard Wollheim, *The Thread of Life* [Cambridge: Harvard University Press, 1984], 198).

4. Søren Kierkegaard, *Either/Or* vol. 2, trans. David F. Swenson and Lillian Marvin Swenson, rev. paperback edition (Princeton: Princeton University Press), 1971), 264.

5. *Ibid*, 264.

6. An interesting parallel may be observed between Kierkegaard's depiction of aesthetic despair and Hegel's description of the passage from the abstractive consciousness of Stoicism to the unhappy consciousness of Skepticism as "the actual experience of what the freedom of thought is" (G. W. F. Hegel, *Phenomenology of Spirit*, trans. A. V. Miller [Oxford: Oxford University Press, 1952 and 1977], par. 202).

7. Kierkegaard, 265.

8. Søren Kierkegaard, *Concluding Unscientific Postscript*, trans. David F. Swenson and Walter Lowrie (Princeton: Princeton University Press, 1941 and 1974), 176.

9. Kierkegaard, *Either/Or*, 218.

10. Kierkegaard, *Concluding Unscientific Postscript*, 289.

11. Søren Kierkegaard, *The Sickness Unto Death*, in *Fear and Trembling and The Sickness Unto Death*, trans. Walter Lowrie (Garden City, N.Y.: Doubleday Anchor, 1954), 30.

12. Robert Denoon Cumming, *Starting Point: An Introduction to the Dialectic of Existence* (Chicago: University of Chicago Press, 1979), 408.

13. David J. Gouwens, "Kierkegaard on the Ethical Imagination," *Journal of Religious Ethics* (Fall 1982): 212–13.

14. It is true that in his later work, *Stages on Life's Way*, he treats justification within the context of the third, religious phase of life, which follows the aesthetic and the ethical. A discussion of this lies outside the scope of the present work, although we might remark that Kierkegaard's method of dealing with this problem would be unacceptable to those of us who think ethics requires autonomous forms of justification. Søren Kierkegaard, *Stages on Life's Way*, trans., Walter Lowrie (London: Oxford University Press, 1945).

15. *Ibid.*, 197.

16. Kant, *Critique of Practical Reason*, 166.

17. A term borrowed from Richard Wollheim, *The Thread of Life* (Cambridge: Harvard University Press, 1984).

18. In his final major work, *Religion Within the Limits of Reason Alone* (trans., T. M. Greene and H. H. Hudson [New York: Harper Torchbooks, 1960], 51), Kant is much more open to the inclinations: "Natural inclinations, *considered in themselves*, are *good*, that is, not a matter of reproach, and it is not only futile to want to extirpate them but to do so would also be harmful and blameworthy . . . only what is opposed to the moral law is evil in itself, absolutely reprehensible, and must be completely eradicated."

19. A detailed study of the metaphorical processes involved in seeing-as is beyond the scope of the present work. See Marcus B. Hester, *The Meaning of Metaphor: An Analysis in the Light of Wittgenstein's Claim that Meaning is Use* (The Hague: Mouton, 1967); Paul Ricoeur, *The Rule of Metaphor: Multi-disciplinary Studies in the Creation of Meaning in Language*, trans. Robert Czerny et al. (Toronto: University of Toronto Press, 1977); Paul Ricoeur, "The Metaphorical Process as Cognition, Imagination, and Feeling," *Critical Inquiry* 5 (1978): 143–59; Mary Schaldenbrand, "Metaphoric Imagination: Kinship Through Conflict," in Charles E. Reagan, ed., *Studies in the Philosophy of Paul Ricoeur* (Athens, Oh.: Ohio University Press, 1979).

CHAPTER 6. THE MORAL PHILOSOPHY OF THE SELF

1. Immanuel Kant, *Critique of Practical Reason* (1788), trans. Lewis White Beck (Indianapolis: Bobbs-Merrill, 1956), 166.

2. *Republic* 439–44, and the allegory of the cave, 514–19. See also the Seventh Letter, trans. B. Jowett. *The Dialogues of Plato*, 2 vols. (New York: Random House, 1937).

3. *Phaedrus* 247–52. Jowett, 251–59.

4. Jan Bremmer, *The Early Greek Concept of the Soul* (Princeton: Princeton University Press, 1983). Bremmer argues that the Greeks distinguished at least two concepts of the psyche: the "free soul" which was individual, but lacked psychological attributes—"the free soul is the individual's nonphysical mode of existence not only after death but also in dreams, swoons, and other types of unconsciousness" (17); and the various forms of body soul (e.g. *thymos, nous,* and *menos*), ranging from the corporeal to the gaseous, which endowed persons with life and consciousness.

5. See Marcia Cavell, "The Self and Some Related Issues: A Philosophical Perspective, Parts 1 & 2," *Psychoanalysis and Contemporary Thought* 8 (1985): 3–28, 29–44.

6. *The Philosophical Works of Descartes*, vol. 1, trans. Elizabeth S. Haldane and G. R. T. Ross (Cambridge: Cambridge University Press, 1969), 150.

7. Locke, John. *An Essay Concerning Human Understanding* (1690), 2 vols. (London: J. M. Dent & Sons, 1961), vol. 1, book 2, ch. 27, section 17, p. 286. Locke later assimilates the "forensic" (i.e., concerned with merit and blame) term "person" to the concept of the self: "*Person*, as I take it, is the name for this *self*. Wherever a man finds what he calls *himself*, there, I think, another may say is the *same person*" (vol. 1, book 2, ch. 27, section 26, p. 291).

8. David Hume, *A Treatise of Human Nature* (1739), ed. L. A. Selby-Bigge (Oxford: Clarendon Press, 1888, 1968), 251.

9. *Ibid*, 252–53.

10. Immanuel Kant, *Critique of Pure Reason*, trans. Norman Kemp Smith (London: MacMillan, 1970), B155–158 (167–69), A341–366 (328–44), B428–430 (380–82). For a thorough discussion of Kant's concept of the self, see C. D. Broad, *Kant: An Introduction* (Cambridge: Cambridge University Press, 1978), ch. 2. See also Richard D. Chessick, "The Problematic Self in Kant and Kohut," *Psychoanalytic Quarterly* 69 (1980): 456–73.

11. Broad, 234.

12. Broad, 250.

13. Charles Taylor, *Sources of the Self: The Making of the Modern Identity* (Cambridge: Harvard University Press, 1989).

14. Immanuel Kant, *Foundations of the Metaphysics of Morals* (1785), trans. Lewis White Beck (Indianapolis: Bobbs-Merrill, 1959), 53

15. Thomas Hobbes, *Leviathan (Or the Matter, Form, and Power of a Commonwealth, Ecclesiastical and Civil)* (1651) (London: Everyman, 1970), 44.

16. Kant's *Lectures on Ethics*, trans. Louis Infield (New York: Harper Torchbook, 1979), 45.

17. This distinction is similar to Aristotle's distinction between efficient (that by which a thing comes into existence) and formal causality (the structural features of a thing which condition its possibilities).

18. Carol Gilligan, *In a Different Voice* (Cambridge: Harvard University Press, 1982).

19. Owen Flanagan, *Varieties of Moral Personality: Ethics and Psychological Realism* (Cambridge: Harvard University Press, 1991).

CHAPTER 7. THE SELF IN CLASSICAL PSYCHOANALYSIS

1. Robert Musil, *The Man Without Qualities* (1930) (London: Picador, 1974), vol. 1., 174–75.

2. See Ernst A. Ticho and Arnold D. Richards, "Psychoanalytic Theories of the Self," *Journal of the American Psychoanalytic Association* 30 (1982): 717–33; Arnold M. Cooper, "The Place of Self Psychol-

ogy in the History of Depth Psychology," in Arnold Goldberg, ed., *The Future of Psychoanalysis* (New York; International Universities Press, 1983); Leo Rangell, "The Self in Psychoanalytic Theory," *Journal of the American Psychoanalytic Association* 30 (1982): 863–91; William I. Grossman, "The Self as Fantasy: Fantasy as Theory," *Journal of the American Psychoanalytic Association* 30 (1982): 919–37; Robert S. Wallerstein, "Self Psychology and 'Classical' Psychoanalytic Psychology: The Nature of Their Relationship," *Psychoanalysis and Contemporary Thought* 6 (1983): 553–95; Robert S. Wallerstein, "The Bipolar Self: Discussion of Alternative Perspectives," *Journal of the American Psychoanalytic Association* 30 (1982): 893–917; W. W. Meissner, "Can Psychoanalysis Find Its Self?" *Journal of the American Psychoanalytic Association* 34 (1986): 379–400; Arnold D. Richards, "The Superordinate Self in Psychoanalytic Theory and in the Self Psychologies," *Journal of the American Psychoanalytic Association* 30 (1982): 939–57; Donald McIntosh, "The Ego and the Self in the Thought of Sigmund Freud," *International Journal of Psychoanalysis* 66 (1985): 95–107; Marcia Cavell, "The Self and Some Related Issues: A Philosophical Perspective, Parts 1 & 2," *Psychoanalysis and Contemporary Thought* 8 (1985): 3–28, 29–44; Dale Boesky, "The Problem of Mental Representation in Self and Object Theory," *Psychoanalytic Quarterly* 52 (1983): 564–83.

3. A good historical coverage of the drive concept in Freudian thought is provided by Alan Compton in "The Current Status of the Psychoanalytic Theory of Instinctual Drives. 1: Drive Concept, Classification, and Development" and 2: The Relation of the Drive Concept to Structures, Regulatory Principles, and Objects," *Psychoanalytic Quarterly* 52 (1983): 364–401, 402–26.

4. See William I. Grossman, "The Self as Fantasy: Fantasy as Theory," *Journal of the American Psychoanalytic Association* 30 (1982): 919–37.

5. See Michael St. Clair, *Object Relations and Self Psychology: An Introduction* (Monterey, Calif.: Brooks/Cole, 1986); A. H. Modell, *Object Love and Reality: An Introduction to the Psychoanalytic Theory of Object Relations* (New York: International Universities Press, 1968); H. Hartmann, *Essays on Ego Psychology: Selected Problems in Psychoanalytic Theory* (New York: International Universities Press, 1964).

6. Jacobson, following Hartmann, defines the self in an all-embracing sense "as referring to the whole person of an individual, including his body and body parts as well as his psychic organization and its parts . . . the "self" is an auxiliary descriptive term, which points ot the person as a subject in distinction from the surrounding world of objects" (E. Jacobson, *The Self and the Object World* [New York: International Universities Press, 1964], 6n).

7. Sigmund Freud, Letter to Fliess, 14 November 1897, quoted in

M. Khan and R. Masrud, *The Privacy of the Self* (London: Hogarth Press), 107.

8. Quoted in Joseph Sandler, Alex Holder, and Dale Meers, "The Ego Ideal and the Ideal Self,' *Psychoanalytic Study of the Child* 18 (1963), 149.

9. See Meissner, 380–81.

10. See Otto F. Kernberg, "Self, Ego, Affects, and Drives," *Journal of the American Psychoanalytic Association* 30 (1982): 895; and Jacob G. Jacobson, "The Structural Theory and the Representational World," *Psychoanalytic Quarterly* 52 (1983): 514.

11. H. Hartmann, "Comments on the Psychoanalytic Theory of the Ego," *Psychoanalytic Study of the Child* 5 (1950): 74–96.

12. H. Hartmann, "The Development of the Ego Concept in Freud's Work" (1956), reprinted in H. Hartmann, *Essays on Ego Psychology* (New York: International Universities Press, 1964). Hartmann's distinction was maintained and developed by E. Jacobson, who treated the ego as a fusion of self-image and object-image ("The Self and the Object World: Vicissitudes of their Infantile Cathexes and their Influence on Ideational and Affective Develpment," *Psychoanalytic Study of the Child* 9 [1954]: 75–127); and L. Spiegel ("The Self, the Sense of Self, and Perception," *Psychoanalytic Study of the Child* 14 (1959): 84–109. For a more recent treatment, see J. G. Jacobson, "The Structural Theory and the Representational World,' *Psychoanalytic Quarterly* 52 (1983): 514–42.

13. According to Meissner, the unresolved ambiguities were more serious.

14. I. Spiegel, "The Self, the Sense of Self, and Perception," *Psychoanalytic Study of the Child* 14 (1959): 84–109; L. Spiegel, "Affects in Relation to Self and Object," *Psychoanalytic Study of the Child* 21 (1966): 69–92.

15. J. Sandler and B. Rosenblatt, "The Concept of the Representational World," *Psychoanalytic Study of the Child* 17 (1962): 128–45; Joseph Sandler, Alex Holder, and Dale Meers, "The Ego Ideal and the Ideal Self," *Psychoanalytic Study of the Child* 18 (1963): 139–58.

16. Sandler and Rosenblatt define introjection as "the vesting of certain object representations with a certain status, so that these are felt to have all the power and authority of the real parents" (Sandler and Rosenblatt, "The Concept of the Representational World," 138) and identification with an object as "the coalescence or fusion of a self-representation and an object representation, or a change in the self-representation, so that the object representation is duplicated" (137).

17. O. F. Kernberg, *Object Relations Theory and Clinical Psychoanalysis* (New York: Aronson, 1976), 57.

18. Otto F. Kernberg, "Self, Ego, Affects, and Drives," *Journal of the American Psychoanalytic Association* 30 (1982): 893–917.

19. See Jacob G. Jacobson, "The Structural Theory and the Representational World," *Psychoanalytic Quarterly* 52 (1983): 525ff.

20. J. Sandler and B. Rosenblatt, "The Concept of the Representational World," 135.

21. Dale Boesky, "The Problem of Mental Representation in Self and Object Theory," *Psychoanalytic Quarterly* 52 (1983), 572.

22. Dale Boesky, "The Problem of Mental Representation in Self and Object Theory," 564–83.

23. W. W. Meissner, "Can Psychoanalysis Find Its Self?" *Journal of the American Psychoanalytic Association* 34 (1986), 385.

24. Meissner's term is "structural model," but this, as Boesky (576) has pointed out, obscures the debate. There are two issues involved here: self as structure vs. self as representation, and self as systemic product vs. self as superordinate identity. Freudians tend to equate structural questions with systemic ones. Kohut advances a conception of self which is structural, but not systemic.

25. George S. Klein, *Psychoanalytic Theory: An Exploration of Essentials* (New York: International Universities Press, 1976). For critiques of Klein's work, see A. Frank, "Two Theories or One? or More?" *Journal of the American Psychoanalytic Association* 27 (1979); 169–207; and Arnold D. Richards, "The Superordinate Self in Psychoanalytic Theory and in the Self Psychologies," *Journal of the American Psychoanalytic Association* 30 (1982): 946.

26. J. E. Gedo, *Beyond Interpretation* (New York: International Universities Press, 1979).

CHAPTER 8. ETHICAL IDEALIZATION IN CLASSICAL PSYCHOANALYSIS

1. Sigmund Freud. "Why War: Letters between Einstein and Freud (1932)," *SE* 22 (London: Hogarth Press, 1964), 205.

2. In its second aspect it came to be treated as the center of an immortality system. See Drew Westen, *Self and Society: Narcissism, Collectivism and the Development of Morals* (Cambridge: Cambridge University Press, 1985), 107–10.

3. Sigmund Freud. "On Narcissism: An Introduction" (1914), *SE* 14, ed. James Strachey (London: Hogarth Press, 1957, 1968), 69–102.

4. *Ibid.*, 100–101.

5. Sigmund Freud. "Group Psychology and the Analysis of the Ego" (1921), *SE* 18: 67–143 (London: Hogarth Press, 1955, 1962), 112–13.

6. Indeed, Spruiell, who is sympathetically concerned to find the unities in Freud's early work on the subject, acknowledges that some of Freud's remarks verge on the contradictory. See Spruiel, 781.

7. V. Spruiell, "Freud's Concept of Idealization," *Journal of the American Psychoanalytic Association* 27 (1979): 778.

8. Freud, *On Narcissism," passim.*

9. Ibid., 93–94.

10. Sigmund Freud, *The Ego and the Id* (1923), trans. Joan Riviere (London: Hogarth Press, 1947).

11. See also Sigmund Freud. "Remarks on the Theory and Practice of Dream Interpretation" (1923), *SE* 19 (London: Hogarth Press, 1961): " . . . we should keep firmly to the fact that the separation of the ego from an observing critical, punishing agency (an ego ideal) must be taken into account in the interpretation of dreams as well."

12. *Ibid.,* 47–48.

13. H. Nunberg, *Principles of Psychoanalysis* (New York: International Universities Press, 1955). I am indebted to the survey by Sandler and colleagues for this and the next four citations.

14. A. Reich, "Early Identifications as Archaic Elements in the Superego," *Journal of the American Psychoanalytic Association* 2 (1954).

15. E. Jacobson, "The Self and the Object World: Vicissitudes of Their Infantile Cathexes and Their Influence on Ideational and Affective Development," *Psychoanalytic Study of the Child* 9 (1954).

16. G. Piers and M. B. Singer, *Shame and Guilt* (New York: W. W. Norton, 1953).

17. J. Lample-de-Groot, "Ego Ideal and SuperEgo," *Psychoanalytic Study of the Child* 17 (1962).

18. Heinz Hartmann and Rudolf M. Loewenstein, "Notes on the Superego," *Psychoanalytic Study of the Child* 17 (1962): 42–81, see esp. 58ff. See also his earlier "Comments on the Psychoanalytic Theory of the Ego," *Psychoanalytic Study of the Child* 5 (1950): 74–96.

19. See J. Sandler, A. Holder, and D. Meers, "The Ego Ideal and the Ideal Self," *Psychoanalytic Study of the Child* 18 (1963), 145.

20. Heinz Hartmann, *Psychoanalysis and Moral Values* (New York. International Universities Press, 1960), 50.

21. *Ibid.,* 53.

22. Sigmund Freud. "The Future of an Illusion" (1927), *SE* 21 (London: Hogarth Press, 1964), 295.

23. See Joseph Sandler, Alex Holder, and Dale Meers, "The Ego Ideal and the Ideal Self," *Psychoanalytic Study of the Child* 18 (1963), 149.

24. See Charles Hanly, "Ego Ideal and Ideal Ego," *Internat. J. Psychoanal.* 65 (1984): 255.

CHAPTER 9. HEINZ KOHUT'S PSYCHOANALYTIC SELF PSYCHOLOGY

1. Heinz Kohut, *The Restoration of the Self* (New York: International Universities Press, 1977), 116.

2. Heinz Kohut, *The Analysis of the Self* (New York: International Universities Press, 1971); *The Restoration of the Self* (New York: International Universities Press, 1977); *How does Analysis Cure?*, ed. Arnold Goldberg, with the collaboration of Paul Stepansky (Chicago: University of Chicago Press, 1984).

3. Arnold Richards, not a supporter of Kohut, calls his new theory of the self "the one most likely to threaten the cohesion of the psychoanalytic community" (Arnold D. Richards, "The Superordinate Self in Psychoanalytic Theory and in the Self Psychologies," *J. Amer. Psychoanal. Assn.* 30 (1982): 950.

4. H. Hartmann, "Comments on the Psychoanalytic Theory of the Ego," *Psychoanalytic Study of the Child* 5 (1950): 85ff.

5. H. Kohut and E. S. Wolf, "The Disorders of the Self and their Treatment: An Outline," *Internat. J. Psychoanal.* 59: 414.

6. *Restoration*, 215–16.

7. Sigmund Freud, "Recommendations to Physicians Practising Psycho-Analysis" (1912), *SE* 12 (London: Hogarth Press, 1957), 115. Kohut notes (*Restoration* 255) that Freud's informally expressed views were often far more moderate.

8. Kohut, *Restoration*, 259. See also 302ff.

9. *Restoration*, 311.

10. Leo Rangell, "The Self in Psychoanalytic Theory," *Journal of the American Psychoanalytic Association* 30 (1982): 878.

11. As mentioned earlier, this is a somewhat shifting term. Rangell includes as its proponents people who others, such as Wallerstein, characterize as its opponents. (For example, Jacobson, Sandler and Rosenblatt, and Kernberg.)

12. *Ibid*, 887.

13. Robert S. Wallerstein, "Self Psychology and 'Classical' Psychoanalytic Psychology: The Nature of Their Relationship," *Psychoanalysis and Contemporary Thought* 6 (1983): 590.

14. *Ibid*, 591.

15. C. Brenner, "The Components of Psychic Conflict and its Consequences in Mental Life," *Psychoanal. Quarterly* 48 (1979): 563. Quoted in Wallerstein, 567.

16. C. Hanly, "Narcissism, Defense, and the Positive Transference." Paper presented to Feb. 1982 meeting of the San Francisco Psychoanalytic Society. Quoted in Wallerstein, 566.

17. J. Sandler, "Psychological Conflict and the Structural Model:

Some Clinical and Theoretical Implications," *Internat. J. Psychoanal.* 55 (1974): 53–62.

18. T. Dorpat, "Structural Conflict and Object Relations Conflict," *Journal of the American Psychoanalytic Association* 24 (1976): 855–74.

19. *Ibid*, 856.

20. P. H. Ornstein, "Self Psychology and the Concept of Health," in Arnold Goldberg, ed., *Advances in Self Psychology* (New York: International Universities Press, 1980).

21. Wallerstein, 576.

22. *Ibid.*, 577.

23. *Ibid.*, 577.

24. N. Treuniet, "Psychoanalysis and Self Psychology: A Metapsychological Essay with a Clinical Illustration," *J. Amer. Psychoanal. Assn.* 31 (1983): 87. Quoted in Wallerstein, 582.

25. Wallerstein, 582.

26. According to Boesky, Sandler and Kernberg are "widely viewed as utilizing representational theory within the structural point of view" (566).

27. Heinz Kohut. *How does Analysis Cure?* ed. Arnold Goldberg, with the collaboration of Paul Stepansky. Chicago: University of Chicago Press, 1984.

28. Ernst A. Ticho, "The Alternate Schools and the Self," *Journal of the American Psychoanalytic Association* 30 (1982).

CHAPTER 10. NARCISSISM AND
ETHICAL IDEALIZATION IN SELF PSYCHOLOGY

1. Gaston Bachelard. *The Poetics of Space*, tran. from the French by Maria Jolas, with a foreword by Etienne Gilson (Boston: Beacon Press, 1969 [1964]), 195.

2. Heinz Kohut, "Forms and Transformations of Narcissism" (1966), in Paul Ornstein, ed., *The Search for Self: Selected Writings of Heinz Kohut, 1950–1978*, vol. 1 (New York: International Universities Press, 1978), 427–60.

3. For a more recent characterization of the developmental process, see Richard D. Chessick, *Psychology of the Self and the Treatment of Narcissism* (Northvale, N.J.: Aronson, 1985), 157–60.

4. Heinz Kohut, *The Analysis of the Self* (New York: International Universities Press, 1971), 187.

5. *Ibid.* 50–51.

6. Heinz Kohut, "Summarizing Reflections," in Arnold Goldberg, ed., *Advances in Self Psychology* (New York: International Universities Press, 1980), 539–40.

7. Heinz Kohut, *The Restoration of the Self* (New York: International Universities Press, 1977), 132–33.

8. Kohut, *Restoration*, 243.

9. Richard D. Chessick, *Psychology of the Self and the Treatment of Narcissism* (Northvale, N.J.: Aronson, 1985), 7.

10. R. Spitzer, *Diagnostic and Statistical Manual of Mental Disorders*, 3d ed. (Washington, D.C.: American Psychiatric Association, 1980), 315–17.

11. Chessick, *Psychology of the Self*, 134ff.

12. Charles Kligerman, "Art and the Self of the Artist," ed. Arnold Goldberg, *Advances in Self Psychology*.

13. Charles B. Strozier, "Heinz Kohut and the Leadership Relation," in Goldberg, *Advances*.

14. Randall C. Mason, "The Psychology of the Self: Religion and Psychotherapy," in Goldberg, *Advances*, 407–26.

15. Lynn F. Greenlee, Jr. "Kohut's Self Psychology and the Theory of Narcissism: Some Implications Regarding the Fall and Restoration of Humanity," *Journal of Psychology and Theology* 14 (1986): 110–16.

16. Kohut, *Restoration*, 63.

17. Kohut, *Restoration*, 229.

18. Sigmund Freud, *The Ego and the Id* (1923), 4th ed., trans. Joan Riviere (London: Hogarth Press, 1947), 49–50.

19. *Restoration*, 227–28.

20. See Masrud Khan, *The Privacy of the Self* (London: Hogarth Press, 1974), 192.

21. Heinz Kohut, "Summarizing Reflections," in Goldberg, *Advances*, 511.

22. *Ibid.*, 481.

23. *Ibid.*, 509.

24. Cf. Kohut's internalization of empathy, in *Restoration*, 100.

25. Immanuel Kant, *Anthropology from a Pragmatic Point of View*, trans. Mary J. Gregor (The Hague: Martinus Nijhoff, 1974), 30.

26. Immanuel Kant, *Foundations of the Metaphysics of Morals*, trans. Lewis White Beck (Indianapolis: Bobbs Merrill, 1976), 61.

27. To this end, Kohut develops the idea of "concretized thought": "The greatest steps made in the history of science—the pioneering experiments of the greatest scientists—are thus, as I said earlier, sometimes 'not primarily arrangements designed to facilitate discovery or to test hypotheses' but 'concretized thought'; or put more correctly, they are 'action thought,' a precursor to thinking" (Kohut, *Restoration*, 300).

28. *Ibid.*, 281ff.

CHAPTER 11. MORAL AUTHORITY FOR A FREE PEOPLE

1. William Wordsworth, *Prelude* XIV:188–92, in *William Wordsworth: Selected Poetry*, ed. Mark Van Doren (New York: Modern Library, 1950), 387.

2. Immanuel Kant, *Foundations of the Metaphysics of Morals*, trans., Lewis White Beck (Indianapolis: Bobbs Merrill, 1976), 45

3. *Ibid.*, 59.

4. *Ibid.*, 65.

5. *Ibid.*, 67.

6. *Ibid.*, 69.

7. *Ibid.*, 70.

8. *Ibid.*, 70.

9. Historically, it has tended to be used to describe reason or will controlling wild passions, or in Buddhist and Stoic notions of escape from those passions. See also Spinoza's notion of freedom of consciousness, which is autonomy not in thinking what you want, but thinking what you must (*Ethics* 4, propositions 67–73).

10. E. D. Watt, *Authority* (London & Canberra: Croom Helm, 1982), 11ff.

11. This point is usefully elaborated by Winch in "The Universalizability of Moral Judgments," in Peter Winch, *Ethics and Action* (London: Routledge & Kegan Paul, 1972).

12. *Restoration*, 82–83.

13. For a careful (but I think overly pessimistic) view of the apparently frequent lack of relation between virtue, mental health, and happiness, see Owen Flanagan, *Varieties of Moral Personality: Ethics and Psychological Realism* (Cambridge: Harvard University Press, 1991), ch.15.

14. Aristotle. *Nichomachaen Ethics*, 1106b29–34, trans. Terrence Irwin (Indianapolis: Hacket, 1985).

15. *Ethics*, 1107a10–12.

16. *Ethics*, 1105b2–4.

17. Alasdair MacIntyre, *After Virtue*, 2d ed. (Notre Dame, Ind.: University of Notre Dame Press, 1984).

18. *Ethics*, 1099b.1–5.

19. *Ethics*, 1140b.8.

20. *Ethics* 1104b.5–7.

21. *Ethics*, 1099a.16–18.

22. Aristotle. *De Anima III* 431a.17, Richard McKeon, *The Basic Works of Aristotle* (New York: Random House, 1941).

23. The debate over obscurities in Aristotle's concept of imagination is one of the more heated controversies in Aristotelian scholarship. See Michael V. Wedin, *Mind and Imagination in Aristotle* (New Haven: Yale University Press, 1988); White, Kevin. "The Meaning of *Phantasia* in Aristotle's *De Anima III,3–8, Dialogue* 24 (1985): 483–505; Malcome F. Lowe, "Aristotle on Kinds of Thinking," *Phronesis* 28 (1983): 17–30.

24. Aristotle, *Ethica Eudemia* 1114a31–b1, quoted in Wedin, 98.

25. *Ethics*, 1103a.1.

26. For much of structuralist and post-structuralist theory, the self, *qua* reflexive awareness at the center of experience and action, is a concept which has outlived its meaning. According to Corngold, "the main tendency of the new French criticism [Barthes, Beneviste, Foucault, Lacan, Levi-Strauss] is an attack on the self as it has been understood since German Idealism as the agent of its own development." Stanley Corngold, *The Fate of the Self: German Writer and French Theory* (New York: Columbia University Press, 1986), 4.

27. Rene Descartes, *Discourse on the Method of Rightly Conducting the Reason and Seeking for Truth in the Sciences*, in *The Philosophical Works of Descartes*, vol. 1, trans. Elizabeth S. Haldane and G. R. T. Ross (Cambridge: Cambridge University Press, 1969), 91.

BIBLIOGRAPHY

Arbib, Michael A., and Mary B. Hesse, *The Construction of Reality*. Cambridge: Cambridge University Press, 1986.

Aristotle. *Nichomachean Ethics*. Translated by Terrence Irwin. Indianapolis: Hackett, 1985.

———. *Basic Works*. Edited by Richard McKeon. New York: Random House, 1941.

Babbitt, Irving. *On Being Creative and Other Essays*. Boston: Houghton Mifflin, 1932.

Bachelard, Gaston. *The Poetics of Space*. New York: Orion Press, 1964.

Barrrett, William. *Irrational Man: A Study in Existential Philosophy*. Garden City, N.Y.: Doubleday Anchor, 1962.

Bell, Gordon H. "Imagination and Moral Education." *Journal of Moral Education* 8 (1978): 99–109.

Bernstein, Richard J. *Beyond Objectivism and Relativism: Science, Hermeneutics, and Praxis*. Philadelphia: University of Pennsylvania Press, 1983.

Block, Ned. *Readings in Philosophy of Psychology*. 2 vols. Cambridge: Harvard University Press, 1981.

———. *Imagery*. Cambridge: MIT Press, 1981.

Boesky, Dale. "The Problem of Mental Representation in Self and Object Theory." *Psychoanalytic Quarterly* 52 (1983): 564–83.

Bossart, W. H. "Sartre's Theory of the Imagination." *Journal of the British Society of Phenomenology* 11 (1980): 37–53.

Breen, Hal J. "A Psychoanalytic Approach to Ethics." *Journal of the American Academy of Psychoanalysis* 14 (1986): 255–75.

Bremmer, Jan. *The Early Greek Concept of the Soul*. Princeton: Princeton University Press, 1983.

Brenner, C. "The Components of Psychic Conflict and Its Consequences in Mental Life." *Psychoanalytic Quarterly* 48 (1979): 547–67.

Brightman, Edgar Sheffield. *A Philosophy of Ideals*. New York: Henry Holt, 1928.

Broad, C. D. *Kant: An Introduction*. Cambridge: Cambridge University Press, 1978.

Bundy, Murray Wright. *The Theory of Imagination in Classical and Medieval Thought*. Chicago: University of Chicago Press, 1927.

Campbell, Thomas Douglas. *Adam Smith's Science of Morals*. London: Allen and Unwin, 1971.

Cascardi, Anthony J., ed. *Literature and the Question of Philosophy.* Baltimore: Johns Hopkins University Press, 1987.

Casey, John. "Emotion and Imagination." *Philosophical Quarterly* 34 (1984): 1–14.

Casey, Edward S. *Imagining: a Phenomenological Study.* Bloomington: Indiana University Press, 1976.

———. "Sartre on Imagination." *The Philosophy of Jean-Paul Sartre.* Edited by Paul Arthur Schilpp. 139–66

Cavell, Marcia. "The Self and Some Related Issues: A Philosophical Perspective, Parts 1 & 2." *Psychoanalysis and Contemporary Thought* 8 (1985): 3–28, 29–44.

Chambliss, J. J. *Imagination and Reason in Plato, Aristotle, Vico, Rousseau, and Keats.* The Hague: Martinus Nijhoff, 1974.

Chessick, Richard D. "The Problematic Self in Kant and Kohut." *Psychoanalytic Quarterly* 69 (1980): 456–73.

———. *Psychology of the Self and the Treatment of Narcissism.* Northvale, N.J.: Jason Aronson, 1985.

———. "A Comparison of the Notions of Self in the Philosophy of Heidegger and the Psychoanalytic Self Psychology of Kohut." *Psychoanalysis and Contemporary Thought* 11 (1988): 117–44.

Collingwood, R. G. *Principles of Art.* Oxford: Clarendon Press, 1938.

Compton, Alan. "The Current Status of the Psychoanalytic Theory of Instinctual Drives 1: Drive Concept, Classification and Development." *Psychoanalytic Quarterly* 52 (1983): 364–401

———. "The Current Status of the Psychoanalytic Theory of Instinctual Drives 2: The Relation of the Drive Concept to Structures, Regulatory Principles, and Objects." *Psychoanalytic Quarterly* 52 (1983): 402–26.

———. "The Concept of Identification in the Work of Freud, Ferenczi, and Abraham: a Review and Commentary." *Psychoanalytic Quarterly* 54 (1985): 200–33.

Cooper, Arnold M. "The Place of Self Psychology in the History of Depth Psychology." In *The Future of Psychoanalysis.* Edited by Arnold Goldberg. New York: International University Press, 1983.

Corngold, Stanley. *The Fate of the Self: German Writers and French Theory.* New York: Columbia University Press, 1986.

Crawford, Donald W. "Kant's Theory of Creative Imagination." *Essays in Kant's Aesthetics.* Chicago: University of Chicago Press, 1982.

Cumming, Robert Denoon. *Starting Point: An Introduction to the Dialectic of Existence.* Chicago: University of Chicago Press, 1979.

Dancy, Jonathan. "The Role of Imaginary Cases in Ethics." *Pacific Philosophical Quarterly* 66 (1985): 141–53.

Danto, Arthur C. "Philosophy as/and/of Literature." *Literature and the Question of Philosophy.* Edited by Anthony Cascardi. Baltimore: Johns Hopkins University Press, 1987.

————. "Concerning Mental Pictures." *Journal of Philosophy* (Janaury 1958): 12–20.

Dauer, Francis Watanabe. "Between Belief and Fantasy: A Study of the Imagination." Unpublished paper, 1987.

Davidson, Donald. "On the Very Idea of a Conceptual Scheme." *Proceedings and Addresses of the American Philosophical Association* 47 (1973–74): 5–20.

DeMarco, Joseph. "The Role of Ideals: a Model for Applied Ethics." *Philosophy in Context* 13 (1983): 45–51.

Dent, N. J. H. *The Moral Psychology of the Virtues.* Cambridge: Cambridge University Press, 1984.

Descartes, René. *Discourse on Method and the Meditations.* F. E. Sutcliffe, trans. Harmondsworth, Middlesex, England: Penguin Books, 1977.

————. "Discourse on the Method of Rightly Conducting the Reason and Seeking for Truth in the Sciences." In *The Philosophical Works of Descartes,* vol. 1. Translated by Elizabeth S. Haldane and G. R. T. Ross. Cambridge: Cambridge University Press, 1969.

————. "Third Set of Objections with Author's Reply." In *Philosophical Works,* vol. 2. Translated by Elizabeth Haldane and G. R. T. Ross. Cambridge: Cambridge University Press, 1967.

Dilman, Ilham. "Imagination." *Proceedings of the Aristotelian Society Supplement* 41 (1967): 19–36.

Dorpat, T. "Structural Conflict and Object Relations Conflict." *Journal of the American Psychoanalytic Association* 24 (1976): 855–74.

Dutton, Dennis, and Michael Krausz, eds. *The Concept of Creativity in Science and Art.* The Hague: Martinus Nijhoff, 1981.

Edel, Abraham. *Method in Ethical Theory.* Indianapolis: Bobbs-Merrill, 1963.

Engell, James. *The Creative Imagination: Enlightenment to Romanticism.* Cambridge: Harvard University Press, 1981.

Flanagan, Owen. *Varieties of Moral Personality.* Cambridge: Harvard University Press, 1991.

Foot, Philppa. "Morality and Art." *Proceedings of the British Academy* 56 (1970): 131–44.

Frank, A. "Two Theories or One? or More?" *Journal of the American Psychoanalytic Association* 27 (1979): 169–207.

Freud, Sigmund. "The Ego and the Id" (1923). *Standard Edition* 19. London: Hogarth Press, 1947.

————. "New Introductory Lectures on Psychoanalysis" (1932 [1923]). *Standard Edition* 22. London: Hogarth Press, 1964.

————. "Group Psychology and the Analysis of the Ego" (1921). *Standard Edition* 18: 67–143. London: Hogarth Press, 1955, 1962.

————. "Why War: Letters between Einstein and Freud" (1932). *Standard Edition* 22. London: Hogarth Press, 1964.

————. "On Narcissim: an Introduction" (1914). *Standard Edition* 14: 69–102. Edited by James Strachey. London: Hogarth. Press, 1957, 1968.

————. "Remarks on the Theory and Practice of Dream Interpretation" (1923). *Standard Edition* 19. London: Hogarth Press, 1961.

————. "Recommendations to Physicians Practising Psycho-Analysis" (1912). *Standard Edition* 12: 109–20. London: Hogarth Press, 1957.

————. "The Future of an Illusion" (1927). *Standard Edition* 21. London Hogarth Press, 1964.

Furlong, E. J. *Imagination*. London: Allen & Unwin, 1961.

Gadamer, Hans-Georg. *Truth and Method*. New York: Crossroads, 1982.

Gardiner, Patrick. "German Philosophy and the Rise of Relativism." *Monist* 64: (1981), 138–53.

Gauthier, David. *Morals by Agreement*. Oxford: Clarendon Press, 1986.

Gedo, J. E. *Beyond Interpretation*. New York: International Universities Press, 1979.

Goldberg, Arnold, ed. *Advances in Self Psychology*. New York: International Universities Press, 1980.

————. *The Future of Psychoanalysis*. New York: International Universities Press, 1983.

Goldman, Alvin I. *Philosophical Applications of Cognitive Science*. Boulder: Westview Press, 1993.

Gombrich, E. H. *Art and Illusion: A Study in the Psychology of Pictorial Representation*. Princeton, N.J.: Princeton University Press, 1969.

Gore, W. C. *The Imagination in Spinoza and Hume*. Chicago: University of Chicago Press, 1902.

Gouwens, David J. "Kierkegaard on the Ethical Imagination." *Journal of Religious Ethics*, vol. 10, no. 2 (Fall 1982).

Greenlee, Lynn F., Jr. "Kohut's Self Psychology and the Theory of Narcissism: Some Implications Regarding the Fall and Restoration of Humanity." *Journal of Psychology and Theology* 14 (1986): 110–16.

Grossman, William I. "The Self as Fantasy: Fantasy as Theory." *Journal of the American Psychoanalytic Association* 30 (1982): 919–37.

Hampshire, Stuart. *Morality and Conflict*. Oxford: Blackwell, 1983.

————. *Thought and Action*. New York: Viking Press, 1960.

————. "Commitment and Imagination." In Northrop Frye, Stuart Hampshire, Connor Cruise O'Brien, *The Morality of Scholarship*. Edited by Max Black. Ithaca, N.Y.: Cornell University Press, 1967.

Hanly, Charles. "Ego Ideal and Ideal Ego." *International Journal of Psychoanalysis* 65 (1984): 253–61.

————. "Narcissism, Defense, and the Positive Transference." Paper presented to Feb. 1982 meeting of the San Francisco Psychoanalytic Society.

Hare, R. M. *Moral Thinking: Its Levels, Method, and Point.* Oxford: Clarendon Press, 1981.

Hargreaves, H. L. "The 'Faculty' of the Imagination." *British Journal of Psychology*, Monograph Supplement 3 (1927): 1–74.

Harman, Gilbert. "Moral Relativism Defended." *Philosophical Review* 34 (1975): 3–22.

Hartmann, Heinz. *Psychoanalysis and Moral Values.* New York: International Universities Press, 1960.

———. "Comments on the Psychoanalytic Theory of the Ego." *Psychoanalytic Study of the Child* 5 (1950): 74–96.

———. *Essays on Ego Psychology: Selected Problems in Psychoanalytic Theory.* New York: International Universities Press, 1964.

———. "The Development of the Ego Concept in Freud's Work" (1956): reprinted In H. Hartmann, *Essays on Ego Psychology.* New York: International Universities Press, 1964.

Hartmann, Heinz, and Rudolf M. Loewenstein. "Notes on the Superego." *Psychoanalytic Study of the Child* 17 (1962): 42–81.

Hegel, G. W. F. *Phenomenology of Spirit.* Translated by A. V. Miller. Oxford: Oxford University Press, 1952, 1977.

Hempel, Carl G. "The Theoretician's Dilemma: A Study in the Logic of Theory Construction." *Minnesota Studies in the Philosophy of Science* 2 (1958): 37–98.

Hennessy, John W., and Bernard Gert. "Moral Rules and Moral Ideals: A Useful Distinction in Business and Professional Practice." *Journal of Business Ethics* 4 (1985): 105–16.

Hester, Marcus B. *The Meaning of Metaphor: An Analysis in the Light of Wittgenstein's Claim that Meaning Is Use.* The Hague: Mouton, 1967.

Hoffman, Robert R. "Some Implications of Metaphor for Philosophy and Psychology of Science." In *The Ubiquity of Metaphor: Metaphor in Language and Thought.* Edited by Wolf Paprotte and René Dirven. Amsterdam Studies in the Theory and History of Linguistic Science IV: Current Issues in Linguistic Theory, vol. 29. Amsterdam/Philadelphia: John Benjamins Publishing Company, 1985.

Hollis, Martin, and Steven Lukes, eds. *Rationality and Relativism.* Cambridge: MIT Press, 1984.

Howard, Robert W. *Concepts and Schemata: An Introduction.* London: Cassell, 1987.

Paprotte, Wolf, and René Dirven, eds. *The Ubiquity of Metaphor: Metaphor in Language and Thought.* Amsterdam Studies in the Theory and History of Linguistic Science IV: Current Issues in Linguistic Theory, vol. 29. Amsterdam/Philadelphia: John Benjamins Publishing Company, 1985.

Hume, David. *A Treatise of Human Nature*, 1739. Edited by L. A. Selby-Bigge. Oxford: Clarendon Press, 1968.

Ishiguro, Hide. "Imagination." *British Analytical Philosophy*. Edited by Bernard Williams and Alan Montefiore. London: Routledge & Kegan Paul, 1966.

———. "Imagination." *Proceedings of the Aristotelian Society*. Supplement 41 (1967): 37–56.

Jacobson, E. "The Self and the Object World: Vicissitudes of their Infantile Cathexes and their Influence on Ideational and Affective Development." *Psychoanalytic Study of the Child* 9 (1954): 75–127.

———. *The Self and the Object World*. New York: International Universities Press, 1964.

Jacobson, Jacob G. "The Structural Theory and the Representational World." *Psychoanalytic Quarterly* 52 (1983): 514–42.

James, William. "What Makes a Life Significant." In William James, *Talks to Teachers on Psychology and to Students on Some of Life's Ideals*, 1899. Cambridge: Harvard University Press, 1983.

Johnson, Mark. *The Body in the Mind: The Bodily Basis of Meaning, Imagination, and Reason*. Chicago: University of Chicago Press, 1987.

———. "Imagination in Moral Judgement." *Philosophy and Phenomenological Research* (Dec. 1985): 265–80.

———. *Moral Imagination: Implication of Cognitive Science for Ethics*. Chicago: University of Chicago Press, 1993.

Johnson, Mark, ed. *Philosophical Perspectives on Metaphor*. Minneapolis: University of Minnesota Press, 1981.

Johnson, Mark L., and Glenn W. Erickson. "Toward a New Theory of Metaphor." *Southern Journal of Philosophy* 18 (1980): 289–99.

Johnson, Samuel. *The Rambler*. 3 vols. Edited by W. J. Bate and Albrecht B. Strauss. New Haven: Yale University Press, 1969. Vol. 2, no. 89 (22 Jan. 1751) and no. 125 (28 May 1751).

Kant, Immanuel. *The Doctrine of Virtue* (Part 2 of *The Metaphysics of Morals*). Translated by Mary J. Gregor. Philadelphia: University of Pennsylvania Press, 1964.

———. *Critique of Judgement*. Translated by J. H. Bernard. New York: Haffner Press (Macmillan), 1951.

———. *Critique of Pure Reason*. Translated by Norman Kemp Smith. London: Macmillan, 1970.

———. *Religion within the Limits of Reason Alone* Translated by T. M. Greene and H. H. Hudson. New York: Harper Torchbooks, 1960.

———. *Foundations of the Metaphysics of Morals*. Translated by Lewis White Beck. Indianapolis: Bobbs Merrill, 1976.

———. *Anthropology from a Pragmatic Point of View*. Translated by Mary J. Gregor. The Hague: Martinus Nijhoff, 1974.

———. *Critique of Pure Practical Reason*. Translated by Lewis White Beck. Translated by Indainapolis: Bobbs-Merrill, 1956.

————. *Lectures on Ethics*. Translated by Louis Infield. New York: Harper Torchbook.

Kaufmann, Walter, ed. and trans. *Existentialism from Dostoevsky to Sartre*. New York: New American Library, 1975.

Kekes, John. "Feeling and Imagination in Metaphysics." *Idealistic Studies* vol. 7, no. 1 (Jan. 1977): 76–93.

Kernberg, Otto F. "Self, Ego, Affects, and Drives." *Journal of the American Psychoanalytic Association* 30 (1982): 893–917.

————. *Object Relations Theory and Clinical Psychoanalysis*. New York: Aronson, 1976.

Khan, M. Masud. R. *The Privacy of the Self*. London: Hogarth Press, 1974.

Kierkegaard, Søren. *Stages on Life's Way*. Translated by Walter Lowrie. London: Milford, Oxford University Press, 1945.

————. *The Sickness Unto Death*. In *Fear and Trembling and The Sickness Unto Death*. Translated by Walter Lowrie. Garden City, N.Y.: Doubleday Anchor, 1954.

————. *Either/Or*. 2 vols.. Translated by David F. Swenson and Lillian Marvin Swenson. Revised paperback edition. Princeton: Princeton University Press, 1971.

————. *Concluding Unscientific Postscript*. Translated by David F. Swenson and Walter Lowrie. Princeton: Princeton University Press, 1941 and 1974.

Kittsteiner, H. D. "Kant and Casuistry." Edmund Leites, ed. *Conscience and Casuistry in Early Modern Europe*. Cambridge: Cambridge University Press, 1988.

Klein, George S. *Psychoanalytic Theory: An Exploration of Essentials*. New York: International Universities Press, 1976.

Klinger, Eric. *Structure and Functions of Fantasy*. New York: Wiley Interscience, 1971.

Kohut, Heinz. *The Restoration of the Self*. New York: International Universities Press, 1977.

————. *The Analysis of the Self*. New York: International Universities Press, 1971.

————. "Summarizing Reflections." In *Advances in Self Psychology*. Edited by Arnold Goldberg. New York: International Universities Press, 1980.

————. "Forms and Transformations of Narcissism" (1966). In *The Search for Self: Selected Writings of Heinz Kohut, 1950–1978*, vol. 1, pp. 427–60. Edited by Paul Ornstein. New York: International Universities Press, 1978.

————. "Narcissism as a Resistance and as a Driving Force in Psychoanalysis" (1970). In *The Search for Self*, vol. 2. Edited by P. Ornstein, pp. 554–55. New York: International Universities Press, 1978.

———. *How does Analysis Cure?* Edited by Arnold Goldberg, with the collaboration of Paul Stepansky. Chicago: University of Chicago Press, 1984.

Kohut, H., and E. S. Wolf. "The Disorders of the Self and their Treatment: An Outline." *International Journal of Psychoanalysis* 59: 413–25.

Kosslyn, Stephen Michael. *Image and Mind*. Cambridge: Harvard University Press, 1980.

Lample-de-Groot, J. "Ego Ideal and SuperEgo." *Psychoanalytic Study of the Child* 17 (1962).

Larmore, Charles. "Moral Judgement." *Review of Metaphysics* (Dec. 1981): 275–96.

———. *Patterns of Moral Complexity*. Cambridge: Cambridge University Press, 1987.

Leddy, Thomas Winter. "Imagination, Metaphor, and Cognition: Inside the Concept." *Dissertation Abstracts International* 43 (1983): 3937A. Boston University.

Leites, Edmund, ed. *Conscience and Casuistry in Early Modern Europe*. Cambridge: Cambridge University Press, 1988.

Lloyd, Dan Edward. "Picturing." *Dissertation Abstracts International* 44 (1983): 192A. Columbia University.

Lobkowicz, Nicholas. *Theory and Practice: History of a Concept from Aristotle to Marx*. Lanham, Md.: University of Notre Dame Press, 1967.

Locke, John. *An Essay Concerning Human Understanding 1690*. 2 vols. London: J. M. Dent & Sons, 1961.

London, Nathaniel J. "An Appraisal of Self Psychology." *International Journal of Psychoanalysis* 66 (1985): 95–107.

Loughran, James N. "The Moral Ideal of the Person." *International Philosophical Quarterly* 26 (1986): 147–59.

MacIntyre, Alasdaire. "Relativism, Power and Philosophy." *Proceedings and Addresses of the American Philosophical Association* 59 (1985).

———. *After Virtue*. 2d ed. Notre Dame, Ind.: University of Notre Dame Press, 1984.

Mackay, Alfred. "Extended Sympathy and Interpersonal Utility Comparisons." *Journal of Philosophy* (June 1986).

Mackey, James P., ed. *Religious Imagination*. Edinburgh: Edinburgh University Press, 1986.

McFall, Lynne. "Happiness, Rationality and Individual Ideals." *Review of Metaphysics* 37 (1984): 595–614.

McFarland, Thomas. *Originality and Imagination*. Baltimore: Johns Hopkins University Press, 1985.

McIntosh, Donald. "The Ego and the Self in the Thought of Sigmund Freud." *International Journal of Psychoanalysis* 67 (1986): 429–48.

Meissner, W. W. "Can Psychoanalysis Find Its Self?" *Journal of the American Psychoanalytic Association* 34 (1986): 379–400.

Mercer, Philip. *Sympathy and Ethics.* Oxford: Clarendon Press, 1972.

Miall, David S. *Metaphor and Transformation: The Problem of Creative Thought.* University of Illinois Center for the Study of Reading, report no. 300. Supt. of docs. no. ED1.310 / 2:237958. Cambridge, Mass.: Bolt, Beranek and Newman, 1983.

Mish'alani, James K. "On Moral Imagination." *Man and World* 13 (1980): 193–206.

Mitchell, W. J. T. "What Is an Image?" *New Literary History* (Spring 1984): 503–37.

Modell, A. H. *Object Love and Reality: An Introduction to the Psychoanalytic Theory of Object Relations.* New York: International Universities Press, 1968.

Morrison, Andrew. "Shame, Ideal Self, and Narcissism." *Contemporary Psychoanalysis* 19 (1983): 295–318.

Murray, Edward L. *Imaginative Thinking and Human Existence.* Pittsburgh, Pa.: Duquesne University Press, 1986.

Musil, Robert. *The Man Without Qualities (1930).* 3 vols. London: Picador, 1974.

Nietzche, Friedrich. *Thus Spake Zarathustra.* In *The Portable Neitzche.* Translated by Walter Kaufmann. New York: Viking, 1954.

Novey, S. "The Role of the Superego and Ego Ideal In Character Formation." *International Journal of Psychoanalysis* 36: (1955).

Nunberg, H. *Principles of Psychoanalysis.* New York: International Universities Press, 1955.

Nussbaum, Martha Craven. "Finely Aware and Richly Responsible: Literature and the Moral Imagination." In *Literature and the Question of Philosophy.* Edited by Anthony Cascardi. Baltimore: Johns Hopkins University Press, 1987.

Ornstein, Paul. "Self Psychology and the Concept of Health." In *Advances in Self Psychology.* Edited by Arnold Goldberg. New York: International Universities Press, 1980.

————, ed. *The Search for Self: Selected Writings of Heinz Kohut, 1950–1978,* vol. 1. New York: International Universities Press, 1978.

Paivio, Allan. *Mental Representations: A Dual Coding Approach.* New York: Oxford University Press, 1986.

Paprotte, Wolf, and René Dirven, eds. *The Ubiquity of Metaphor: Metaphor in Language and Thought.* Amsterdam Studies in the Theory and History of Linguistic Science IV: Current Issues in Linguistic Theory, vol. 29. Amsterdam/Philadelphia: John Benjamins Publishing Company, 1985.

Paton, Herbert James. *Kant's Metaphysic of Experience: a Commentary on the First Half of the Critique of Pure Reason.* London: Allen & Unwin, 1970.

Philips, Michael. "Reflections on the Transition from Ideal to Non-Ideal Theory." *Nous* 19 (1985): 551–70.

Piers, G., and M. B. Singer. *Shame and Guilt*. New York: W. W. Norton, 1953.

Pinker, Steven, and Stephen M. Kosslyn. "Theories of Mental Imagery." In *Imagery: Current Theory, Research and Application*. Edited by Anees A. Sheikh. New York: John Wiley & Sons, 1983.

Plato. *Phaedrus*. Translated by B. Jowett. In *The Dialogues of Plato*. 2 vols. New York: Random House, 1937.

Polanyi, Michael. "The Creative Imagination." *Psychological Issues* 6 (1969): 53–91.

Price, Martin. *Forms of Life: Character and Moral Imagination in the Novel*. New Haven: Yale University Press, 1983.

Putnam, Hilary. *Realism and Reason*. Cambridge: Cambridge University Press, 1983.

———. *Reason, Truth and History*. Cambridge: Cambridge University Press, 1981.

———. *Mind, Language and Reality*. Cambridge: Cambridge University Press, 1975.

———. "Why Reason Can't be Naturalized." *Synthese* 52 (1982).

———. "No Ready Made World." *Synthese* 51 (1982).

———. "Three Kinds of Scientific Rationality." *Philosophical Quarterly* 32 (1982).

Rangel, Leo. "The Self in Psychoanalytic Theory." *Journal of the American Psychoanalytic Association* 30 (1982): 863–91.

Reagan Charles E., and David Stewart. *The Philosophy of Paul Ricoeur: An Anthology of His Work*. London: Beacon Press, 1978.

Reagan, Charles E. *Studies in the Philosophy of Paul Ricoeur*. Athens, Oh.: Ohio University Press, 1979.

Reddiford, G. "Moral Imagining and Children." *Journal of Moral Education* 10 (2): 75–85.

Reich, A. "Early Identifications as Archaic Elements in the Superego." *Journal of the American Psychoanalytic Association* 2 (1954).

Ribot Th[eodule Armand]. *Essay on the Creative Imagination*. Chicago: Open Court, 1906. Reprinted by Arno Press, New York, 1973.

Richards, Arnold D. "The Superordinate Self in Psychoanalytic Theory and in the Self Psychologies." *Journal of the American Psychoanalytic Association* 30 (1982): 939–57.

Richards, Ivor Armstrong. *Coleridge on Imagination*. London: Routledge & Kegan Paul, 1955.

Ricoeur, Paul. *The Rule of Metaphor* (translation of *La Métaphore vive*,1975). Translated by Robert Czerny. Toronto: University of Toronto Press, 1977.

———. "The Hermeneutical Function of Distanciation." *Philosophy Today* 17 (1973): 129–41.

———. *Hermeneutics and the Human Sciences: Essays on Language, Action and Interpretation.* Edited, translated, and introduced by John B. Thompson. Cambridge: Cambridge University Press, 1981.

———. "The Metaphorical Process as Cognition, Imagination, and Feeling." *Critical Inquiry* (Autumn 1978): 143–59.

———. "Sartre and Ryle on the Imagination." *The Philosophy of Jean-Paul Sartre.* Edited by Paul Arthur Schilpp. 167–78.

———. "Ideology and Utopia as Cultural Imagination." *Being Human in a Technological Age.* Edited by Donald Borchert. 107–26. Athens, Oh.: Ohio University Press, 1979.

———. "The Function of Fiction in Shaping Reality." *Man and World* 12 (1979): 193–206.

Rossi, Philip J. "Moral Interest and Moral Imagination in Kant." *Modern Schoolman* 57 (1980): 149–58.

Russow, Lilly Marlene. "A Theory of Imagination." *Dissertation Abstracts International* 37 (1976): 2949A. Princeton University.

Ryle, Gilbert. *The Concept of Mind.* New York: Barnes and Noble Books, 1949.

Sandler, J. "Psychological Conflict and the Structural Model: Some Clinical and Theoretical Implications." *International Journal of Psychoanalysis* 55 (1974): 53–62.

Sandler, J., and B. Rosenblatt. "The Concept of the Representational World." *Psychoanalytic Study of the Child* 17 (1962): 128–45.

Sandler, Joseph., Alex Holder, and Dale Meers. "The Ego Ideal and the Ideal Self." *Psychoanalytic Study of the Child* 18 (1963): 139–58.

Sartre, Jean-Paul. *The Psychology of the Imagination.* 2d paperback ed. New York: Citadel Press, 1963. Translated from the French (*L'Imagination, Psychologie Phenomenologique de l'Imagination*). Paris: Galimaud, 1940.

———. *Being and Nothingness.* New York: Philosophical Library, 1956.

Savile, Anthony. "Imagination and Pictorial Understanding." *Aristotelian Society Supplement* 60 (1986): 19–44.

Schafer, R. *A New Language for Psychoanalysis.* New Haven: Yale University Press, 1976.

Schaldenbrand, Mary. "Metaphoric Imagination: Kinship through Conflict." *Studies in the Philosophy of Paul Ricoeur.* Edited by Charles E. Reagan. Athens, Oh.: Ohio University Press, 1979.

Scheler, Max. *The Nature of Sympathy.* London: Routledge & Kegan Paul, 1954.

Scruton, Roger. *Art and Imagination: A Study in the Philosophy of Mind.* London: Routledge & Kegan Paul, 1974.

Seung, T. K. *Semiotics and Thematics in Hermeneutics.* New York: Columbia University Press, 1982.

Sheikh, Anees A., ed. *Imagery: Current Theory, Research and Application*. New York: John Wiley & Sons, 1983.

Sheikh, Anees A., and Katharina S. Sheikh, eds. *Imagery in Education: Imagery in the Educational Process*. Farmingdale, N.Y.: Baywood, 1985.

Shorter, J. M. "Imagination." *Mind* 41 (1952). Reprinted in *Essays in Philosophical Psychology*, 154–70. Edited by Donald Gustavson. Garden City: Doubleday Anchor Books, 1964.

Smith, Adam. *Theory of Moral Sentiments*, 2d ed., 1761. London: Henry G. Bohn, 1853, 3–4.

Smith, Norman Kemp. *A Commentary to Kant's "Critique of Pure Reason."* 2d ed., 1923.

Spiegel, L. "Affects in Relation to Self and Object." *Psychoanalytic Study of the Child* 21 (1966): 69–92.

———. "The Self, the Sense of Self, and Perception." *Psychoanalytic Study of the Child* 14 (1959): 84–109.

Spitzer, R., Chairperson. *Diagnostic and Statistical Manual of Mental Disorders*, 3d ed. Washington, D.C.: American Psychiatric Association, 1980.

Spruiell, Vann. "Freud's Concept of Idealization." *Journal of the American Psychoanalytic Association* 27 (1979): 777–91.

St. Clair, Michael. *Object Relations and Self Psychology: An Introduction*. Monterey, Calif.: Brooks/Cole, 1986.

Strawson, P. F. "Imagination and Perception." *Experience and Theory*. Edited by Lawrence Foster and J. W. Swanson. Amherst: University of Massachusetts Press, 1970.

Strawson, P. F. "Social Morality and Individual Ideal." *Philosophy* (Jan. 1961): 1–17.

Streminger, G. "Hume's Theory of Imagination." *Hume Studies* (Nov. 1980): 98–118.

Taylor, Charles. *Sources of the Self: The Making of the Modern Identity*. Cambridge: Harvard University Press, 1989.

Ticho, Ernst A. "The Alternate Schools and the Self." *Journal of the American Psychoanalytic Association* 30 (1982).

Ticho, Ernst A., and Arnold D. Richards. "Psychoanalytic Theories of the Self." *Journal of the American Psychoanalytic Association* 30 (1982): 717–33.

Treuniet, N. "Psychoanalysis and Self Psychology: A Metapsychological Essay with a Clinical Illustration." *Journal of the American Psychoanalytic Association* 31 (1983).

Tuvson, Ernest Lee. *The Imagination as a Means of Grace: Locke and the Aesthetics of Romanticism*. Berkeley: University of California Press, 1960.

Tyson, Phyllis, and Robert Tyson. "Narcissism and Superego Development." *Journal of the American Psychoanalytic Association* 32 (1984): 75–98.

Wallerstein, Robert S. "Self Psychology and 'Classical' Psychoanalytic Psychology: The Nature of Their Relationship." *Psychoanalysis and Contemporary Thought* 6 (1983): 553–95.

———. "The Bipolar Self: Discussion of Alternative Perspectives." *Journal of the American Psychoanalytic Association* 29 (1979): 377–94.

Walsh, William. *The Use of Imagination: Educational Thought and the Literary Mind*. New York: Barnes and Noble, 1960.

Warnock, Mary. *Imagination*. Berkeley: University of California Press, 1976.

Watt, E. D. *Authority*. London & Canberra: Croom Helm, 1982.

Wedin, Michael V. *Mind and Imagination in Aristotle*. New Haven: Yale University Press, 1988.

Westen, Drew. *Self and Society: Narcisssim, Collectivism and the Development of Morals*. Cambridge: Cambridge University Press, 1985.

White, David A. "On Bridging the Gulf Between Nature and Morality in the Critique of Judgement." *Journal of Aesthetics and Art Criticism* 38 (1979): 179–88.

Wilkerson, T. E. "Seeing-As." *Mind* 82 (1973): 481–96.

Winch, Peter. "The Universalizability of Moral Judgments." In Peter Winch, *Ethics and Action*. London: Routledge & Kegan Paul, 1972.

Wittgenstein, Ludwig. *Philosophical Investigations*. Translated by G. E. M. Anscombe. Oxford: Basil Blackwell, 1968.

Wollheim, Richard. "The Good Self and the Bad Self: The Moral Psychology of British Idealism and the English School of Psychoanalysis Compared." *Proceedings of the British Academy* LXI (1975): 373–98.

———. "Identification and Imagination." *Freud: A Collection of Critical Essays*. Edited by Richard Wollheim. New York: Anchor Books, 1974, 172–95.

———. *The Thread of Life*. Cambridge: Harvard University Press, 1984.

Woods, Michael. "Kant's Transcendental Schematism." *Dialectica* 37 (1983): 201–20.

NAME INDEX

SUBJECT INDEX